English and Oriental Carpets
at Williamsburg

*THE WILLIAMSBURG
DECORATIVE ARTS SERIES*

GRAHAM HOOD, *Editor*

The Williamsburg Collection of Antique Furnishings

New England Furniture at Williamsburg

English and Oriental Carpets at Williamsburg

Northeast bedchamber of the George Wythe House showing No. 10 in place.

English and Oriental Carpets at Williamsburg

By Mildred B. Lanier

Published by
THE COLONIAL WILLIAMSBURG FOUNDATION
Williamsburg, Virginia
Distributed by THE UNIVERSITY PRESS OF VIRGINIA
Charlottesville, Virginia

LIBRARY OF CONGRESS CATALOGING IN PUBLICATION DATA

Lanier, Mildred B   1915-
  English and oriental carpets at Williamsburg.

  (The Williamsburg decorative arts series)
  Bibliography: p.
    1. Rugs, English—Catalogs. 2. Rugs, Oriental—Catalogs.
  3. Rugs—Williamsburg, Va.—Catalogs.
  I. Title. II. Series.
NK2843.L36   746.7'5   74-75782
ISBN 0-8139-0582-6 (University Press of Virginia)

Colonial Williamsburg ISBN: 0-87935-021-0

PRINTED IN THE UNITED STATES OF AMERICA

Contents

Foreword

COLONIAL WILLIAMSBURG has a superb, encyclopaedic collection of English and American textiles of the seventeenth and eighteenth centuries. It helps to furnish the many "period rooms" in the restored colonial city, and will also furnish, we trust, additional scholarly catalogs. Its great scope provides an invaluable research resource into an often-neglected aspect of colonial life, as well as a virtually unending visual delight. That so many of these beautiful and delicate fabrics have been preserved for future generations is praiseworthy; that they can be studied and understood, and their place in the context of the society that made and used them expounded by publications like this, is equally important.

Among the many categories of this collection are the carpets and carpeting discussed in these pages. They were almost all acquired for exhibition purposes and have been shown, during the last forty years, in various interiors here. That we catalog and reproduce them in this book does not mean that we still believe, in the light of modern research, they are all of the kind found in Virginia in the colonial period. Recent publications on the subject[1] have proved that carpets in the American colonies were relatively scarce. It is apparent that, in the past, we have not only installed far too many carpets in the elegant rooms of recently restored colonial houses, but we have often used the wrong kind. When carpets for which there is evidence here in the eighteenth century (Turkey carpets, English Wiltons, Exeters, Axminsters) were not available, others have been used, principally Caucasian. Yet these are precisely the kind that are not likely to have been found in the colonies, for the Caucasus was not open to trade with the West until the nineteenth century.

One of the educational aims of the Colonial Williamsburg Foundation has always been to elucidate the strictly appropriate antique material by placing it within a wider context. Extensive comparisons with both simpler and richer objects can add immeasurably to our understanding and appreciation. We have tried to build the whole range of our collections on a wide degree of quality, to

---

1. Nina Fletcher Little, *Floor Coverings in New England Before 1850* (Sturbridge, Mass., 1967) and Rodris Roth, *Floor Coverings in 18th-Century America* (Washington, D.C., 1967).

give a deeper understanding of the period. Our carpets—material aspects of a culture that has influenced us so profoundly—and this catalog of them enable us to study and convey in depth one further facet of life in colonial Virginia.

—GRAHAM HOOD
Director of Collections
The Colonial Williamsburg
Foundation

Preface

IN THE WHOLE STUDY OF ART, few objects defy concise attributions more obstinately than Oriental carpets. Opinions conflict on the dating, origin, and authenticity of carpet categories as well as of individual examples. A number of authorities have made widely differing statements about Colonial Williamsburg's collection, as they have about many other collections, public and private. Whenever possible, I have incorporated such views into this catalog, thus affording the student more complete information on the subject.

A detailed study of the historical background of Oriental carpets is not thought to be pertinent here, and no attempt has been made to cover that complex subject, especially since most of the carpets illustrated herein date no earlier than the late seventeenth century. The reader is instead referred to the many scholarly works on the subject that are listed in the bibliography. Some of the more representative carpets in the collection are shown in accurate color plates (positioned vertically—as they were woven), with captions that call the reader's attention to features of construction and design and will, I hope, help him understand the complexities involved in accurately assigning date and provenance.

Among the scholars to whom I am most indebted, Dr. Maurice S. Dimand, curator emeritus of Islamic Art, Metropolitan Museum of Art, has assisted in the cataloging of the collection over a period of many years. His scholarly works on Islamic arts are well-known sources of information for the carpet enthusiast. Dr. May H. Beattie of Sheffield, England, has contributed invaluable information on comparative differences in carpet features and other material developing from recent concentrated studies of a vast number of carpets in museums in all parts of the world. Her scholarly research, monographs, and lectures have greatly enlarged our knowledge of the use of Eastern carpets in western Europe in the seventeenth and eighteenth centuries. At John Graham's request, she and Charles Ellis made a study of this collection in 1968, and much of their expertise and descriptive parlance has been utilized in the compilation of this catalog. Charles Grant Ellis, research associate of the Textile Museum, Washington, D.C., author, and lecturer, has given patient assistance and much information stemming from his extensive travels and careful personal scrutiny of many carpets.

I am also deeply grateful to Mary R. M. Goodwin, Colonial Williamsburg research associate, for invaluable information pertaining to colonial furnishings; and to many others including John M. Graham II, curator emeritus, under whose guidance the collection was acquired, and Graham Hood, director of collections, without whose encouragement and gentle prodding this catalog might never have been completed. Colonial Williamsburg photographers Delmore Wenzel and Hans Lorenz skillfully provided photographs of excellent quality.

The writer is entirely sympathetic with the sentiment expressed by Elijah Bemiss in his introduction to *The Dyer's Companion:*

> I shall leave all to itself, and to every man liberty to approve or disapprove as he pleases, and however they determine the author will not be much troubled, for he is certain no man can have a lighter esteem for him, than he has for himself; he however, will be well pleased if any man shall find benefit by what he has written.[1]

MILDRED BOYLE LANIER

A NOTE TO THE READER:

The width (weft) measurement is given first in each caption.

The following construction abbreviations are used throughout the catalog:

Two single yarns spun in the Z (/) direction and plied (twisted together) in the S (\ ) direction will be indicated as Z2S; another way to denote this would be / /\ . Z4S would indicate four Z-spun yarns plied in S twist (/ / / /\ ); the coarse yarn resulting might be referred to as a "fat" yarn (see No. 41).

The number of knots per inch in the weft direction is denoted as h. (horizontal); the number of rows per inch in the warp direction as v. (vertical). In some instances the knot count will be irregular and the average horizontally and vertically will be denoted (h. 6–8, v. 6–7, 36 to 56 knots per square inch).

---

1. Elijah Bemiss, *The Dyer's Companion.* 2d edn. (New York: Evert Duyckinck, 1815), p. 105.

Short-Title List

Bode-Kühnel   Wilhelm von Bode and Ernst Kühnel, *Antique Rugs from the Near East,*
                       translated by Charles Grant Ellis, 4th rev. edn. (Braunschweig, 1958)

Dilley   Arthur Urbane Dilley, *Oriental Rugs and Carpets*, revised by Maurice S.
                       Dimand (Philadelphia, 1959)

Ellis   Charles Grant Ellis. "Mixed Thoughts on Oriental Carpets," *Catalogue
                       of The Delaware Antiques Show* (Wilmington, 1969)

Erdmann (1962)   Kurt Erdmann, *Oriental Carpets*, translated by Charles Grant Ellis (New
                       York, 1962)

Erdmann (1970)   Kurt Erdmann, *Seven Hundred Years of Oriental Carpets*, translated by
                       May H. Beattie and Hildegard Herzog, edited by Hanna Erdmann (Lon-
                       don, 1970)

Kendrick   A. F. Kendrick, *English Decorative Fabrics of the 16th to 18th Centuries*
                       (Benfleet, England, 1934)

Kendrick and Tattersall   A. F. Kendrick and C. E. C. Tattersall, *Hand-Woven Carpets, Oriental
                       and European* (New York, 1922)

Mayorcas   M. J. Mayorcas, *English Needlework Carpets* (Leigh-on-Sea, England,
                       1963)

Tattersall and Reed   C. E. C. Tattersall and Stanley Reed, *A History of British Carpets*, rev.
                       edn. (Leigh-on-Sea, England, 1966)

English Carpets

Seventeenth-Century Turkey-Work

T HE ENGLISH, being more than any other people on earth captivated by foreign novelties,[1] set about duplicating the technique of manufacturing Turkish carpets shortly after the latter reached England in the early sixteenth century. This British manufacture, called Turkey-work for obvious reasons, employed the so-called Turkish or Ghiordes knot (see Fig. 7, page 61).

Throughout the sixteenth and seventeenth centuries and well into the eighteenth, the use of carpet was generally confined to covering tables, chests, and cupboards. Turkey-work made in sizes adaptable for chair covering was so widely used that during the 1680s, when the Eastern novelty of chair caning became popular, the anxious wool manufacturers protested to Parliament on behalf of the Turkey-work chairmakers.[2]

Many references to Turkey-work chairs and carpets appear in late seventeenth- and early eighteenth-century inventories and other records of the southern colonies. At times, even then, these were described as old: the 1701 inventory of Elizabeth Leightonhouse of York County, Virginia, listed "six turkey worke chares old . . . ," and in 1732 the estate of Robert "King" Carter of Corotoman, Lancaster County, Virginia, included "in the Brick House Loft . . . 4 old Turkey workt chairs, 1 large oyle cloth to lay under a Table." The 1692 inventory of Mrs. Elizabeth Digges of York County included two Turkey-work carpets, nine Turkey-work chairs, and a Turkey-work couch. The House of Burgesses specified on April 9, 1703, that "there be provided to be set in the Councill Chamber one Oval table fourteen foot long and six broad with two doz: arm'd Cain Chairs, one large ditto, twenty five green Cushions for the said Chairs stuft with hair, and a large Turky work Carpet for the table."[3]

Turkey-work chairs continued to appear in southern inventories into the

---

1. Philip Stubbes, *Anatomie of the Abuses in Ailgna* (1583), referred to by Therle Hughes, *English Domestic Needlework 1660–1860* (New York, 1961), p. 30.
2. Hughes, p. 33.
3. *Journals of the House of Burgesses of Virginia, 1702–1712*, 4:29–30.

late eighteenth century. This practice of using old, even antique, furniture is indicated by the Reverend Michael Smith, "late of the city of Williamsburg, but now in London," in a letter published in the *London Daily Advertiser* for September 3, 1770, and reprinted in the *Virginia Gazette* (Rind, ed.) on November 29, 1770. Smith attacked the second Virginia nonimportation association for restricting only items "such as scarce are ever imported in that colony . . ." and continued with this pertinent statement: "Not but there are many of the eminent planters whose houses are pretty well furnished; but as much of that furniture is of an hundred years date, so it would serve an hundred years hence, whether there had been an association or not. . . ."[4]

The number of extant sixteenth- and seventeenth-century knotted carpets now known to be English is considerable. Although these carpets were woven and knotted in the same manner as the rare and expensive Turkish or Turkey carpets imported from the East, the English-made examples differed in several fundamental ways. The English carpet knotter substituted linen or hemp for the plied wools used as warp in carpets manufactured in Turkey or the cotton warps primarily used in Persian rugs. The English emulated the Turkish knot (see Fig. 7, page 61), but generally (based on extant examples) used fewer knots to the square inch. Examples owned by the duke of Buccleuch at Boughton House and in the Victoria and Albert Museum indicate, however, that very fine quality was achieved in some English-made carpets of this early period. In the examples at Boughton House, traditional Turkish designs have been skillfully copied, but with a linen warp and a single silk weft shoot, including in the border the arms of Sir Edward Montagu, for whom they were made.[5] However, in the Turkey-work chairs at Williamsburg (Nos. 1–3), English designs and coloring are recognizable, and they are typical of the examples that might have been found in colonial homes.

The manufacture of Turkey-work, which had flourished for about a hundred years, noticeably diminished in the later years of the seventeenth century, probably because of the increased importation of Turkish and other Eastern carpets and partly because of the growing sophistication of home-furnishing styles. The easy chair and other more comfortable upholstered furniture then coming into use required less-bulky materials, such as leather and the strong and vibrantly colored English worsted upholstery goods—moreens, cambletts, harrateens, serges, satins, and damasks. The manufacture of Turkey-work further declined with the increased

4. Quoted by Mary R. M. Goodwin, "The Colonial Store," Colonial Williamsburg Research Department, MS. report, March 1966, pp. 46–48.
5. Tattersall and Reed, plates 2–4, and p. 27.

production of furnishing silks, as well as the ever-present needlework that for centuries had been made with silks and crewels by English women of all walks of life.

1

TURKEY-WORK CHAIR UPHOLSTERY

England, seventeenth century

SIZE, BACK	24 x 12 in.	
	(61 x 30 cm.)	
SEAT	24 x 20 in.	
	(61 x 51 cm.)	
WARP	Hemp, dark natural, Z4S	
WEFT	Hemp, dark natural, Z4S, one shoot after each row of knots	
PILE	English wool, Turkish knot, 49 knots per square inch	
CONDITION	Probably woven as cushion covers and cut when applied to chair frame	

There appears to have been no uniform development of design in seventeenth-century Turkey-work, and this field pattern of stylized carnations on angular strapwork stems is related to English curvilinear embroidery designs. The border shows Eastern influence in the reciprocal angular interlacings and in the arrow-like border guards, which are not included on the other two examples in the catalog (Nos. 2 and 3). The introduction of Eastern motifs was not unusual, however, some extant pieces being of such convincing Anatolian design as to make their East Anglican or Flemish manufacture a matter of speculation among specialists until a thorough analysis proved their European origin.[1]

PROVENANCE Luke Vincent Lockwood, New York, Connecticut; Parke-Bernet Galleries, New York

1954-375

---

1. Tattersall and Reed illustrate a number of these carpets in plates 2, 3, and 4.

Back

1 *Seat*

2

TURKEY-WORK UPHOLSTERY ON CHAIR
England, late seventeenth century

SIZE, BACK	22 x 12 in.	
	(56 x 30 cm.)	
SEAT	26 x 21 in.	
	(66 x 53 cm.)	
WARP	Linen, natural, Z2S, level	
WEFT	Linen, natural, Z2S, one shoot after each row of knots	
PILE	English wool, Turkish knot, 35 knots per square inch	
CONDITION	Black ground pile deteriorated	

A petition of the English wool manufacturers in 1698 stated that "there were yearly made and Vended in this Kingdom about five thousand dozen of Set-work (commonly called Turkey-Work) Chairs though made in England."[1] This style of chair was in favor in England during the reigns of James I and Charles I, and records of colonial America indicate its use from the late seventeenth to mid-eighteenth century. The knotted fabric of this early upholstery innovation was also used for table carpets, cupboard carpets, and cushions for benches. Worsted tapes, galloons, and fringes, with large round-, oval-, and square-headed brass nails, were customary trimmings.

Tulips, roses, and carnations are stiffly conventionalized in this rather coarse example which, due to the threadbare ground, shows the typical heavy linen web of the knotted pile weave (see No. 2A).

PROVENANCE R. Dyke, Ltd., London

1936-168

---

1. Quoted in G. Bernard Hughes, "The Englishness of Turkey-Work," *Country Life*, February 11, 1965, pp. 309–10.

2

2A *Detail of back section*

3

TURKEY-WORK UPHOLSTERY ON CHAIR

England, second half of the seventeenth century

SIZE, BACK	24 x 13¼ in.	
	(61 x 34 cm.)	
SEAT	28½ x 22½ in.	
	(72 x 57 cm.)	
WARP	Linen, natural, Z2S, level	
WEFT	Linen, natural, Z2S, one shoot after each row of knots	
PILE	English wool, Turkish knot, 49 knots per square inch	
CONDITION	Dark brown (originally black) pile deteriorated	

An unmistakably English pattern of tulips, roses, daffodils, and other flowers and leaves in graceful, symmetrical arrangement covers the ground which, originally black or deep brown, has deteriorated due to the corrosive effects of the iron mordants used in the dyeing (see detail, No. 3A).

A Turkey-work chair at the Victoria and Albert Museum appears to be from the same set,[1] and four others are in the Brooklyn Museum.

PROVENANCE Luke Vincent Lockwood, New York, Connecticut; Parke-Bernet Galleries, New York

1954-374

---

1. G. Bernard Hughes, "The Englishness of Turkey-work," *Country Life*, February 11, 1965, fig. 1.

3

3A *Seat detail*

Needlework

EIGHTEENTH-CENTURY ENGLISH NEEDLEWORK carpets were intended to be used as floor coverings. They were made by individuals with varying degrees of skill, employing the more durable canvas stitches (cross-stitch and tent stitch) and working with good English worsteds on stout linen canvas. Mary Granville, Mrs. Delany, wrote her sister, Mrs. Dewes, in 1751, "Monday, I went to Dublin, was two hours and a half choosing worsteds for a friend in the North, who is working a *fright* of a carpet!"[1] Again in 1752 she wrote Mrs. Dewes from Delville, her home in Ireland, ". . . my candlelight work, is finishing a carpet in double cross-stitch, on very coarse canvass, to go round my bed."[2]

A number of eighteenth-century English embroidered carpets survive. Characteristically the four examples in this catalog (Nos. 4–7) show a profusion of large, naturalistic, full-blown flowers with intricate foliage in the style of contemporary ornament. These carpet designs often include dates and armorial crests.[3]

Unless American women were averse to employing so much time on anything as vulnerable as floor carpets, it is difficult to explain why needlework carpets were not mentioned in household inventories or correspondence here before the nineteenth century. Nor can we suggest that these might have been included among the unidentified "English carpets" frequently listed in individuals' orders and merchants' advertisements for, as domestically made furnishings, they were not likely to have been intended for export.

---

1. Lady Llanover, ed. *The Autobiography and Correspondence of Mary Granville, Mrs. Delany*, 3 vols. (London, 1861), 3:50.
2. Ibid., p. 176. Mrs. Delany's "daylight" work on this particular day was spent painting ". . . twice over the upper figures in the Transfiguration . . ."
3. Other English needlework carpets of importance are illustrated in Tattersall and Reed, frontispiece and pp. 43–44; and Kendrick, plates XLVII, XLVIII, and XLIX.

4

4

NEEDLEWORK CARPET

England, about 1740

SIZE   84 x 122 in.
              (213 x 310 cm.)
MATERIALS   Natural linen canvas, embroidery worsteds
STITCHES   Tent stitch, petit point

The oblong central panel with grapevine tracery contains a shield-shaped cartouche with rope-design border enclosing a basket of naturalistic flowers. The
wide main border is composed of an undulating vine bearing large flowers and
fanciful leaves. The outer border shows an arrangement of tulips enclosed by en-
twined dolphin or cloud-band type figures, forming trefoil leaf-and-daffodil corner motifs.

   Very little restoration has been required on this carpet, which is exhibited as
a seasonal change in the parlor of the Governor's Palace (No. 4A).

PROVENANCE   Sir Charles Welby (on loan to the Victoria and Albert Museum);
              Frank Partridge & Sons, Ltd., London
PUBLISHED   Kendrick, pl. XLIX; C. E. C. Tattersall, *A History of British Car-
              pets* (Benfleet, Essex, England, 1934), pl. XXIV; Tattersall and
              Reed, pl. 43; Mayorcas, plates 26 and 27

                                                              1952-425

4A
*Parlor of Governor's Palace
showing No. 4 in place.*

5

NEEDLEWORK CARPET

England, 1740–65

SIZE   77 x 105 in.
            (196 x 267 cm.)
MATERIALS   Natural linen canvas, embroidery wools
STITCHES   Cross-stitch

The boldly outlined center medallion, dominating the rectangular field and the enclosing spandrels or corner blocks, is filled with seminaturalistic flowers and foliage. The same graceful flower motifs appear on the somewhat faded brick-red ground of the wide border.

Other English needlework carpets dating between 1740 and 1770 show similar medallions with pendant volutes on the vertical axis, possibly adapted from Eastern designs. One such example, in the Lady Lever Art Gallery, Port Sunlight, Cheshire, made about 1740[1] and another in the Metropolitan Museum collection dated 1765[2] appear to share the same prototype or design source as this example.

PROVENANCE   Mayorcas, Ltd., London

1968-649

---

1. Mayorcas, pl. 36.
2. Ibid., pl. 48.

5

6

NEEDLEWORK CARPET

England, eighteenth century

SIZE	66 x 84 in.
	(168 x 213 cm.)
MATERIALS	Wool and silk on linen canvas
STITCHES	Cross-stitch

A heavy link-chain motif outlines the central roundel and corner sections and forms the two border guard bands, while large seminaturalistic flowers fill the medallions and the intervening field. Seven fanciful leaf designs are repeated to form the border, which terminates in a stylized lily at each corner.

PROVENANCE	Edwina, Countess Mountbatten of Burma; S. W. Wolsey, London; Frank Partridge & Sons, London; Ohan Berberyan, New York; Parke-Bernet Galleries
PUBLISHED	*Catalog 1929* (New York: Parke-Bernet Galleries, November 19, 1959), No. 19; Mayorcas, p. 45, pl. 45

1959-383

6

7

NEEDLEWORK CARPET

England, about 1740

SIZE	90 x 99 in. (229 x 252 cm.)
MATERIALS	Embroidery wools on linen canvas
STITCHES	Cross-stitch

The central lozenge-shaped bouquet of naturalistic flowers is enclosed by triangular corner motifs of flower-filled cornucopias. Large roses, hyacinths, carnations, iris, and tulips also form the wide border, the guards being worked in a pattern of classical cymatium.

PROVENANCE   Arditti & Mayorcas, London
PUBLISHED   *Apollo* 68 (May 1958):399, fig. VI; Mayorcas, pl. 37
1958-375

8

NEEDLEWORK CARPET

England, nineteenth century

SIZE	90 x 114 in.
	(229 x 290 cm.)
MATERIALS	Embroidery wools on linen canvas
STITCHES	Cross-stitch, tent stitch
CONDITION	Repaired in some areas

The symmetrically arranged architectural devices that form the field pattern have pinwheel, leaf-cluster, or star-flower motifs. Thistle-and-leaf designs show at the four corners. Floral clusters and rosettes cover the intervening portions of the field. Superimposed in the center of the carpet appear the arms of Great Britain encircled by the Garter and its motto, *Honi soit qui mal y pense.* The wide border has octagonal medallions centered in each side—two enclosing patera and two fleur-de-lis. Naturalistic flowers trail from cornucopias at each corner.

PROVENANCE	Mrs. Coriat of Twatley, Malmesbury, Wiltshire; S. W. Wolsey, London
PUBLISHED	Mayorcas, p. 52, pl. 69

1956-45

8

Carpet Knotting
in the Eighteenth Century

URING THE EARLY YEARS of the eighteenth century carpet knotting in England was virtually forgotten. When circumstances involving two discontented workers of the Savonnerie manufactory at Chaillot, near Paris, led to its reintroduction into England in 1750, carpet knotting was heralded as new and different, completely unrecognized as the Turkey-work of an earlier period.

Encouraged by royal patronage and premiums offered by the Royal Society of Arts, a number of established wool cloth manufacturers began anew the manufacture of knotted carpets in England. The first was Peter Parisot, whose fine carpets, produced at Fulham, were in the style of Savonnerie. After about five years this undertaking failed and in 1755 Claud Passavant purchased the equipment and moved it to Exeter. At least two of Passavant's carpets with the woven inscription EXON and dates 1757 and 1758 are extant.[1] The most prosperous manufactories, however, were those of Thomas Moore of Moorfields and Thomas Whitty of Axminster in Devonshire.

Interest in the classical styles influenced the designs of these floor coverings, and records of the period reveal that architects of prominence—Robert Adam, Wyatt, and Leverton among them—designed carpets, often to match the ceiling decorations of specific rooms in such great houses as Syon, Osterley, Saltram, Harewood House, Strawberry Hill, and Woodhall Park. Many of the carpets made from their cartoons still survive.[2] Thomas Moore of Moorfield was a friend of Robert Adam's and many of the designs created by Adam were executed in Moore's shop. Thomas Chippendale, on the other hand, generally referred his clients to Thomas Whitty's manufactory at Axminster, as he did in 1778 when Sir Edward Knatchbull required a carpet for the drawing room at Mersham-le-

---

1. Tattersall and Reed, plates 17 and 18. An account of the establishment of the English carpet manufacture at Fulham is recorded in the *Gentlemen's Magazine,* August 30, 1754, p. 385.

2. A number of knotted carpets woven for these houses are illustrated in Bertram Jacobs, *Axminster Carpets (Hand-Made), 1755–1957* (Leigh-on-Sea, England, 1970).

Hatch. Nevertheless, Sir Edward paid Thomas Moore of Moorfield £57.12.0 in 1779 for "the Carpet for the drawing-room."[3]

It is logical to assume that many of these knotted carpets, made in England after mid-century, came to America. An interesting reference to one of Moore's carpets is found in Henry Wansey's *An Excursion to the United States of North America in the Summer of 1794* (Salisbury, England, 1798). In describing his visit to William Bingham's elaborate house in Philadelphia, he recognized the carpet as "one of Moore's most expensive patterns."[4] There are scattered references to fine Axminsters or large Exeter carpets, so named for place of manufacture, but more often referred to are Wiltons, Brussels (also made at Wilton), and such other British-made carpets as Scotch, Kilmarnock, and Kidderminster. Many carpets in colonial records are unidentified; some are designated only as English carpets. Stephen West, upholsterer in Annapolis, advertised in the *Maryland Gazette* on June 25, 1752, that he had just imported from London all types of furniture including "Turkey and English Carpets." But we do not know from which of the manufactories William Anderson of London procured for his client, Charles Carroll of Annapolis, the "1 Good English Carpet wth. Lively Colours 12/4 by 14 . . ." specified in Carroll's order of 1766.[5]

Two late eighteenth-century English knotted carpets (Nos. 9 and 10) have been tentatively attributed to Thomas Whitty's manufactory at Axminster. Much is known of the Axminster operation, which continued successfully until a fire in 1828; the growing competition of cheaper machine-made carpets finally bankrupted the firm in the early 1830s. The Axminster manufactory was purchased and the equipment and many of the weavers were transferred to the large factory at Wilton where the tradition of carpet knotting by hand continued until the mid-twentieth century.[6]

None of the carpets made at Axminster was signed. However, many documented carpets made by several generations of Whittys are extant, several having remained in the rooms for which they were designed and woven. Bertram Jacobs in his history of the Axminster carpet states: ". . . fortunately his [Whitty's] creations were so characteristic in many ways, in materials, weave and colouring, that it is feasible, with sufficient experience, to recognize an Axminster carpet."[7]

---

3. Tattersall and Reed, p. 45.
4. Quoted by Ruth Page, "English Carpets and Their Use in America," *Connecticut Antiquarian* 19 (June 1967):18.
5. In "Letters of Charles Carroll, Barrister," *Maryland Historical Magazine*, 36 (September 1941):339.
6. Jacobs, *Axminster Carpets*, p. 59.
7. Ibid., p. 40.

9

9

KNOTTED CARPET

England, possibly Axminster, late eighteenth century

SIZE	166 x 238 in.
	(422 x 605 cm.)
WARP	Wool, natural, Z2S, depressed
WEFT	Linen-flax, grayish, Z, 2 and 3 shoots between rows
PILE	Wool, Z, Turkish knot (h. 4–4½, v. 5–6), 20 to 27 knots per square inch
SELVEDGES	Some repairs in overcasting, original two bundles of three warp ends in light brown wool
ENDS	Top rewoven with new wool fringe added, lower end with narrow apron and warp fringe
CONDITION	Some worn areas repaired in flat stitch instead of reknotting; section cut from right side, reinstated at a later date

The "progressive" field arrangement, designed to be viewed from one end, is strangely different from the more formal, symmetrical arrangement of many of the earlier needlework and Turkish carpets with their central medallions and corner spandrels. This curvilinear design, repeated three times along the vertical

Large dining room of Governor's Palace showing No. 9 in place.

axis, shows a torchlike motif with shield base and baluster stem terminating in a heart-shaped pendant. Branching from this in symmetrical arrangement are large stylized flowers, feathery leaves, and other floral devices which join with another vertical arrangement of lamplike volutes on the outer edges of the field. Oblong and cartouche motifs with floral decoration are linked alternately in the border and terminate in anthemion motifs at the corners. The border guards show a twisted ribbon design.

A section cut from the carpet by a former owner, possibly to fit around a hearth, had been preserved and has been reincorporated in the carpet. It is seasonally displayed in the state dining room at the Governor's Palace in Williamsburg (see No. 9A).

PROVENANCE   Parke-Bernet Galleries, New York

PUBLISHED   *Catalog 1674* (New York: Parke-Bernet Galleries, April 26, 27, and 28, 1956), p. 207; Bertram Jacobs, *Axminster Carpets (Hand-Made), 1755–1957* (Leigh-on-Sea, England, 1970), pl. 27

1956-178

10

KNOTTED CARPET

England, possibly Axminster, late eighteenth or early nineteenth century

SIZE   102 x 166 in.
             (259 x 422 cm.)
WARP   Linen, natural, Z4S
WEFT   Linen, natural, Z2S, 2 to 5 less-than-full shoots[1]
PILE   Wool (3 S-plied strands), Turkish knot, 16 knots per square inch
CONDITION   Several repaired and rewoven areas

Naturalistic roses, peonies, and morning glories in natural colors, symmetrically arranged, form an oblong central medallion and branching corner motifs on the dark aubergine ground. The narrow border, enclosed in simple line guards,

---

1. Reference is to weft shoots which travel less than the full distance from selvedge to selvedge, often forming diagonal lines as in tapestry.

IO

has a series of lozenges alternating with small medallions connected by horizontal lines, similar to the border pattern occurring in another carpet attributed to the Axminster factory.[2]

PROVENANCE   Frank Partridge & Sons, London; Parke-Bernet Galleries, New York

PUBLISHED   *Catalog 1929* (New York: Parke-Bernet Galleries, November 19, 1959), No. 47; Bertram Jacobs, *Axminster Carpets (Hand-Made), 1755–1957* (Leigh-on-Sea, England, 1970), pl. 26

1959-384

---

2. Owned by the Henry Francis du Pont Winterthur Museum, it is illustrated in Tattersall and Reed, pl. 21.

Floor Cloths

DOUBLE-CLOTH carpeting, also known as ingrain, Scotch, Kidderminster, and Kilmarnock (the latter two after the location of their fabrication), was one of Britain's most flourishing manufactures from the mid-eighteenth century until the late nineteenth century or possibly later. It seems to have started at Kidderminster in 1735, although the inventory of Lettice, duchess of Leicester, dated 1634, lists ". . . 3 peices of Kittermister stuff" and "4 carpetts of Kidderminster stuff," establishing the fact that loom-woven carpeting of a simpler variety had been manufactured there in the early seventeenth century.[1]

In double-cloth weaving two cloths are woven simultaneously, one above the other, being interwoven at specified intervals to form an all-over patterned cloth in which the colors, of limited number, are reversible from front to back (see Nos. 11 and 12). These cloths, woven about a yard wide, required considerable skill to prevent the "untacked" design elements from being too extensive and to so arrange the colors of the two separate warp and weft systems as to keep the resulting pattern from appearing too striped.[2] Such prodigious quantities of these flat-woven carpeting fabrics were produced in Scotland that they became known as Scotch carpets. At Kilmarnock in 1824 the more durable triple-cloth carpeting was brought to perfection.[3] Another name associated with this carpeting, especially in America, was ingrain, derived possibly from the fact that the worsted warp, sometimes referred to as the chain, and the worsted or woolen weft materials employed in the manufacture were dyed "in the grain," meaning in the yarn or in the fiber.

Other eighteenth-century floor coverings popular in America were painted floor cloths—those with geometric or fancy patterns built up, layer on layer, with oil paints on wide linen canvas (see Fig. 1). These were often painted by local upholsterers, probably from designs in pattern books such as that shown in Fig. 2. Others were ordered to be made in England and shipped to the colonists, often

---

1. Tattersall and Reed, p. 33.
2. Charles Tomlinson, "The Manufacture of Carpets," in *The Useful Arts and Manufactures of Great Britain*, First Series (London, n.d.), pp. 8–9.
3. C. E. C. Tattersall, *A History of British Carpets* (Benfleet, England, 1934), p. 120.

FIGURE 1. *Office in Peyton Rand House showing reproduction floor cloth in place.*

with disastrous results. Thomas Nelson of Yorktown complained to his agent, John Norton & Sons of London, in 1773: "The Cloth is injur'd by being role'd before the paint was dry."[4] They were at best not substantial, and, other than the reproduction shown in Fig. 1,[5] no examples of the type are included in this collection. It is known, however, that throughout this period painted floor cloths were in general use in Virginia. Joseph Kidd, a Williamsburg upholsterer, advertised in the *Virginia Gazette* (Purdie and Dixon, eds.) on December 28, 1769, that he "fits carpets to any room with the greatest exactness . . . and paints floor cloths." The account books of Daniel Rea and Sons of Boston, for October 21, 1788, note: "John Dubollet, Dr. To Painting a Room and Entry Floor Cloth 35 yds @ 2/8 with Poosey Cat on one and a Leetil Spannel on the other, Frenchman like. £4.3.4."[6]

---

4. Frances Norton Mason, ed., *John Norton & Sons, Merchants of London and Virginia* (Richmond, 1937), p. 348.

5. This example was manufactured in the Colonial Williamsburg paint department from instructions given in Tomlinson, op. cit., "The Manufacture of Floor-cloth," pp. 35–50. The pattern was adapted from an English book of designs for floors by "I. Carwitham Inv[entor] et sc[ulptor] 1739"; the copy owned by Colonial Williamsburg was "Printed for John Bowles at the Black Horse in Cornhill" and includes, as described on the title page, "Various kinds of FLOOR DECORATIONS . . . for Ornamenting the Floors of Halls Rooms, . . . Painted Floor Cloths, in Twenty four Copper Plates."

6. Quoted by Elizabeth A. Ingerman from MS 715 in Baker Library, Cambridge, Massachusetts, in "Winterthur Newsletter," March 26, 1962, p. 15.

FIGURE 2. *Plate* XCIV *from Batty Langley's* THE CITY AND COUNTRY BUILDER'S AND WORKMAN'S TREASURE OF DESIGNS (*London, 1741*).

List carpets, a domestically woven kind of floor covering later known as "rag" or "hit or miss" is another type belonging to the eighteenth century. List— evenly cut or torn strips of cloth—was woven with a strong cotton, linen, or worsted warp on a simple two-harness loom and formed the colorful warp (see Fig. 5) and weft striped patterns characteristic of these carpets. They were often used as protective coverings for more valuable carpets or parquet floors. A surprisingly early mention of them is found in the 1749 inventory of George Charlton of Williamsburg ("a List floor Cloth 7/6"). The Dutch watercolor *Family of Five at Tea*, about 1765–70 (Fig. 3), and the *Family Group* by Hendrik Pothoven (1724–1795) painted during his stay in England (Fig. 4) provide evidence of this practice. Another such *Family Group*, painted by Pothoven in 1774, shows several widths of list carpeting stitched together to make a large rug that appears to partially cover an Oriental carpet.[7] Still another document clearly depicting list carpeting is the 1754 painting by Tibout Regters (1701–1768) of *The Family of Jacob van Stamhorst*.[8]

FIGURE 3. "*Family of Five at Tea*," *watercolor, Dutch, ca. 1770, artist unknown. Colonial Williamsburg Foundation, 1958–632.*

7. Mario Praz, *Conversation Pieces* (London, 1971), p. 215, fig. 175.
8. Ibid., p. 235, fig. 216.

FIGURE 4. *"Family Group,"
oil, Hendrik Pothoven
(1725–1795). Painted during
the artist's stay in England.
Courtesy of Tillou Galleries.*

FIGURE 5. *Detail of American
nineteenth-century list or
Venetian carpeting in which the
closely set multicolored warp
stripes predominate. This
example, from an early
nineteenth-century Pennsylvania
house, illustrates the durable,
narrow carpeting (usually a yard
wide) used extensively for halls
and stairways and often seamed
to make larger room-sized
carpets. Gift of Wade E.
Stonesifer, Baltimore.
G1967-721.*

11

SCOTCH CARPETING

Great Britain, eighteenth or nineteenth century

SIZE   36 in. (91 cm.) loom width
MATERIALS   Worsted

This double-woven worsted carpeting has a pattern of rectangles, octagons, and other plain and diapered geometric forms. Carpeting of this type was also called ingrain, Kilmarnock, or Kidderminster, all of which were usually woven in three-quarter and yard widths, suitable for stair carpeting or, seamed and often bordered, for room-size floor coverings. Worn ingrain carpeting was utilized for other purposes, such as carpetbags or, as shown here, for a horse blanket. The carpeting blanket has a quilted cotton lining and worsted tape trim with leather and brass fastenings, all in rather worn condition.

PROVENANCE Ginsburg & Levy, New York

1968-7

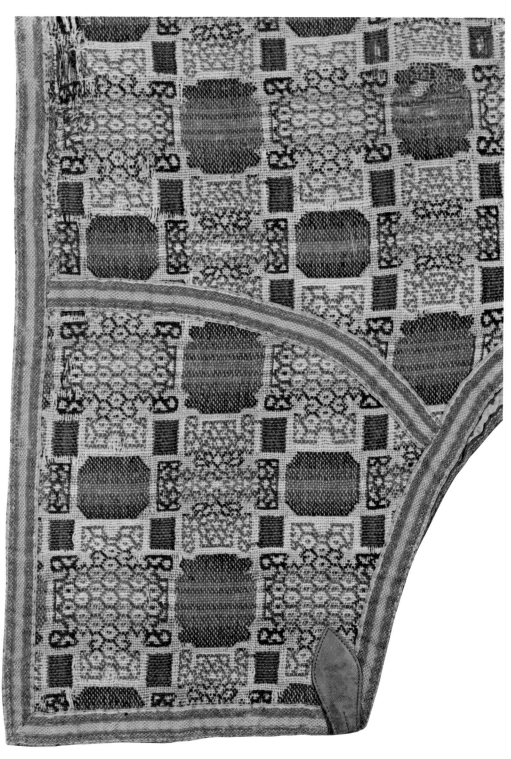

II

12

SCOTCH CARPETING

Great Britain, eighteenth or nineteenth century

SIZE   36 in. (91 cm.) wide
MATERIALS   Wool (worsted double-cloth), tabby-weave

Small patterned, mosaic designs are more durable in this double-woven technique, whereas the "pockets" formed by large patterns are more susceptible to wear. Double-cloths are reversible; this example has light octagons on dark ground on the reverse side.

Parquet and mosaic designs were often specified in floor cloths and carpets, as in the Dublin Society's premium competition for the year 1780, when an award was offered for the "best Irish Carpet . . . in imitation of ancient Mosaic . . . to be made of the Wilton kind."[1]

PROVENANCE   Gift of Mr. John D. Rockefeller 3rd, New York
G1956-297

1. Ada K. Longfield, "History of Carpet-Making in Ireland in the 18th Century," *Journal of the Royal Society of Antiquaries of Ireland* 70 (June 1940):70.

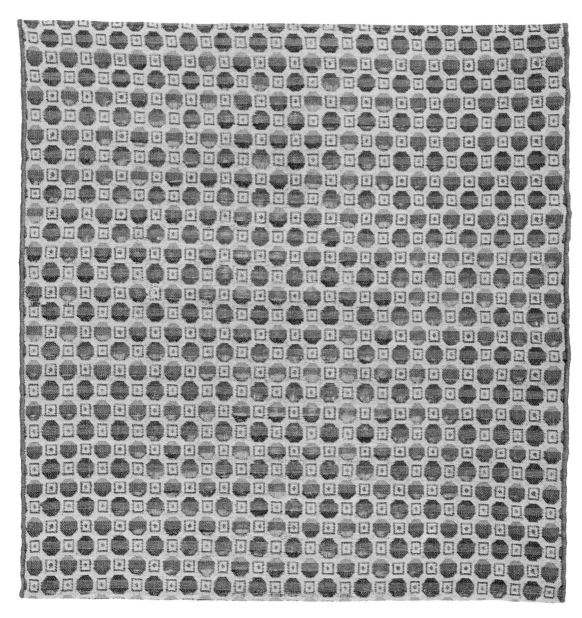

12

13

PRINTED FLOOR CLOTH

Probably America, early nineteenth century

SIZE   126 x 158 in.
            (384 x 401 cm.)
FABRIC
    WIDTH   28–30 in.
            (74–76 cm.)
WARP   Cotton, natural, Z3S
WEFT   Mixed fiber (cotton, wool, linen), natural, Z3S, printed
            in blue, coral, brick, and reserve white
WEAVE   5/1 weft twill

The size and over-all printed design of this weft twill cotton fabric indicate that, although rather light in weight, it was intended as a floor cloth. Since this example appears never to have been used, it might be assumed that varnish or wax was to be applied to the surface after installation to provide body and greater durability as a floor covering.

PROVENANCE   Gift of Mr. and Mrs. Mitchel Taradash, New York
                                                    G1952-15

13

14

TAPESTRY-WOVEN FLOOR CLOTH

Probably England, eighteenth century

SIZE	76 wide (seamed) x 43 in.
	(193 x 109 cm.)
	Fabric 48 in. wide (122 cm.)
WARP	Cotton, natural, Z4S
WEFT	Cotton, salmon, blue, Z4S
WEAVE	Interlocked tapestry, over one, under one

This remnant of sturdily woven cotton floor canvas has salmon and indigo-blue diamond lozenges measuring 5¼ x 7¾ inches in closely interlocked tapestry weave. Possibly much larger originally, the example shows evidence of having been patched up and stenciled over at some time.

PROVENANCE Charles Angell, Bath, England

1956-537

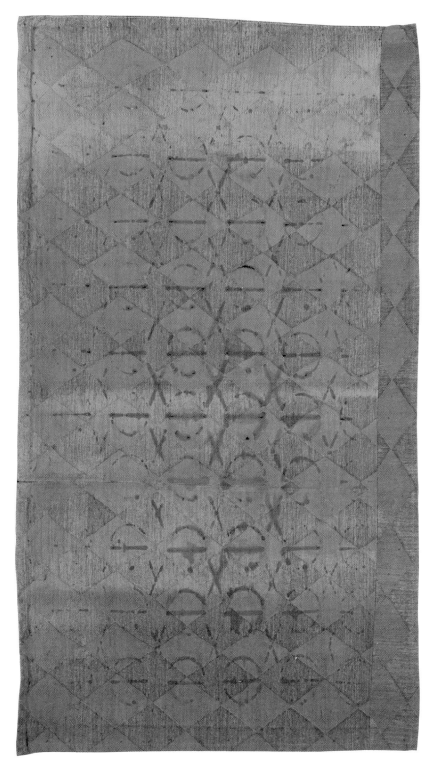

14

Wilton and Brussels Carpeting

FOREIGN VISITORS' COMMENTS attest that carpets were in widespread use in America in the last half of the eighteenth century. Count Brissot de Warville, writing in 1788, appeared indignant at the luxurious display of carpets:

> It already appears: they have carpets, elegant carpets; it is a favourable taste with the Americans; They receive it from the interested avarice of their old masters the English. A carpet in summer is an absurdity; yet they spread them in this season, and from vanity: this vanity excuses itself by saying that the carpet is an ornament; that is to say, they sacrifice reason and utility to show.[1]

When these observations were made, one of the ostentatious status symbols was Wilton carpeting, as records of the time indicate. George Washington wrote to his secretary Tobias Lear in Philadelphia on March 10, 1797: "let me request you to provide for me as usual new Carpeting as will cover the floor of my blue Parlour. That it may accord with the furniture it ought to have a good deal of blue in it; and if Wilton is not much dearer than Scotch carpeting, I would prefer the former. . . . P.S. The parlour is about 18 foot Square, a suitable border if to be had, should accompany the Carpeting. . . ."[2]

Price probably contributed to the popularity of the velvet or plush-pile Wilton and Brussels carpets; less expensive but certainly not as durable as those of knotted construction, they gave somewhat the same effect in a room. John Quincy Adams indicated the popularity of Wilton carpeting:

> And maples, of fair glossy stain,
>   Must form my chamber doors,
> And carpets of the Wilton grain,
>   Must cover all my floors.[3]

---

1. Jacques Pierre Brissot de Warville, *New Travels in the United States of America, Performed in 1788*, 2d edn. (London, 1794), 1:270.
2. John C. Fitzpatrick, ed., *The Writings of George Washington from the Original Manuscript Sources, 1745–1790* (Washington, D.C., 1931–44), 37:577–79.
3. John Quincy Adams, "Wants of Man," *Poems of Religion and Society* (Buffalo, 1854), quoted by Rodris Roth, *Floor Coverings in 18th-Century America* (Washington, D.C., 1967), p. 40, fn. 91.

In 1772, the late Lieutenant Governor Francis Fauquier's inventory listed "1 large Wilton Carpet" valued at £6, while "1 large Turkey Carpet" from the same estate was sold to George Wythe for £5.[4] The former, one supposes, was newer and more fashionable and probably less worn. A "large Wilton Persian carpet" was said to have been owned before the Revolutionary War by Colonel George William Fairfax at Belvoir, his plantation near Mount Vernon.[5] This reference, as well as paintings of the late eighteenth century, indicate the practice of adapting Eastern motifs to the less costly but highly coveted English-made floor covering. Williamsburg owners of valuable Wilton carpets included William Prentis, whose 1765 estate included a Wilton carpet worth £13,[6] and Peyton Randolph, whose inventory of 1776 listed a Wilton carpet valued at £10.[7] A 1775 deed of trust on Tazewell Hall, the Williamsburg home of John Randolph, Peyton's Tory brother, listed with other elegant furnishings "one handsome Wilton carpet, one old Ditto . . . one Wilton Carpet. . . ."[8] Very large carpets, including a Wilton carpet 24 x 18 feet, together with Scotch carpets 20 x 18 and 24 x 18, and "1 painted floor Cloth 20 feet by 18 . . ." were included in an "Invoice for Goods for Joseph Prentis Williamsburg" with note appended "W^msburg Ap^l: 3^d 1780 Mr Beal agrees to join J. Prentis in the risk of importing the above Goods from Curacoa, and to pay half of their amount in Curacoa. . . ."[9] This indicates that English goods, even if by circuitous routes, found their way to America while hostilities continued. The following year, at Morattico Plantation in Lancaster County, Virginia, "1 Large Wilton Carpet £10" was among the valuable "Goods at Mr. Chinns removed there for fear of the Enemy. . . ."[10]

Very few Wilton and Brussels carpets have survived and there are none at Williamsburg. Miss Roth, however, illustrates a late eighteenth- to early nineteenth-century carpet of Wilton construction with a central motif resembling the Great Seal of the United States, owned by the Mount Vernon Ladies Association of the Union.[11] There is also a notable eighteenth-century example of a cut-

---

4. York County, Wills and Inventories, No. 22 (1771–83), p. 95. "An Account Sales of Goods . . . Estate of the Hon. Francis Fauquier, July 20, 1772."

5. Mary Newton Stanard, *Colonial Virginia: Its People and Customs* (Philadelphia, 1917), p. 88.

6. York County, Wills and Inventories, No. 21 (1760–71), pp. 253–63. Inventory of the estate of William Prentis recorded October, 1765.

7. Ibid., No. 22 (1771–83), pp. 337–40. Inventory of the estate of Hon. Peyton Randolph, taken January 5, 1776.

8. The Deed of Trust on Tazewell Hall, Williamsburg, Virginia, to Peyton Randolph, John Blair, and James Cocke, August 26, 1775; MS in Colonial Williamsburg Research Department archives.

9. Webb-Prentis MSS, University of Virginia Library, quoted in Mary R. M. Goodwin, "Carpets, Carpeting, Floor Cloths, Rugs" (MS report, Colonial Williamsburg Research Department, 1960; revised 1966), p. 13.

10. Lancaster County, Wills and Deeds, No. 20 (1770–83), pp. 200–204. Inventory of Rawleigh Downman. This inventory also included "1 Scotch carpet 50/, 2 Tapestry do. and 1 bedside do. 40/.'

11. Roth, *Floor Coverings*, p. 43, fig. 20

pile carpet of striking Persian pattern, tentatively attributed to the Wilton factory, at Governor Tryon's palatial residence at New Bern, North Carolina.

These cut (Wilton) and uncut (Brussels) velvet or plush pile constructions were more easily converted to mechanical loom manufacture than were the more durably constructed knotted pile carpets, and their manufacture continues virtually unchanged to the present day.

Oriental Carpets

Persian Carpets

THE COLONIAL WILLIAMSBURG period would logically preclude mention of Persian carpets, for as U. A. Dilley has written, "The colonists at Jamestown were making cabins out of forests when the last of the great patrons of rugs, Shah Abbas, received the embassies of the kings of Europe upon the court carpets of Ispahan."[1] But as the earliest rug in the collections is early seventeenth century (No. 15), a brief history is warranted here.

Persian carpets before the sixteenth century are known to us only through miniature paintings. As late as the fifteenth century, rug patterns were rather simple geometric designs related to those of Anatolia. Persian carpets (now in museum and private collections) made during the sixteenth century in the Safavid court centers of Tabriz, Kashan, Herat, and Ispahan show a revolutionary change in design. Carpets in the new design, woven from cartoons worthy of the highly respected miniaturists, illuminators, and other artists, include delicately wrought medallion and scroll patterns related to book art, complex curvilinear masterpieces with graceful arabesques, and flower palmettes on artistically interlaced systems of spiraling stems. Many have realistic animals and figures whose intricate detail and symmetry, attained by executing several hundred knots to the square inch, rivaled those drawn by pen or brush. With variations and certain impoverishments, these classic designs have continued in use to the present day.

This golden age of carpet weaving, established by the Safavid rule under Shah Ismail, endowed by the patronage of the powerful Shah Tahmasp (1524-1576) and brought to artistic zenith by his grandson, Shah Abbas I (1588-1629), produced carpets of such magnificent grandeur that they are today numbered among the art treasures of the world. So much in demand were these fine wool and silken treasures as gifts from the shah to royal houses of Europe whom he wished to impress, and later through trade with Europe, that even as they attained perfection their quality began to diminish. Impoverishment of design and workmanship began as early as the last half of the seventeenth century.

---

1. Dilley, p. 279.

Fine carpets were made in the province of Kurdistan in northwest Persia, where village weaving continued into the nineteenth century. This area had close connections with the Caucasus, and similarities are evident in the designs of carpets from the two regions.

In view of the reassessment claiming possible attribution to India of certain so-called Herati carpets,[2] it should be mentioned that Persian influence and craftsmen found their way into the court of the great Mogul emperor of India, Akbar (1556-1605), and that by the last half of the seventeenth century Indian knotted carpets with designs based on the finer and freer patterns of Persia were being exported in considerable numbers.[3]

The majority of Persian carpets employ the "Persian" or "open" knot, which is also called the "Sehna" knot. With this knot it is possible, on the fine silk and cotton warps generally used, to maintain the curvilinear beauty of the naturalistic forms and figures as well as the delicate scroll-work symmetry of the well-ordered secondary patterns.

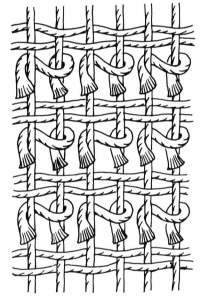

FIGURE 6. *Persian knot with two shoots of weft*

---

2. Discussed in No. 15.
3. Kendrick and Tattersall, pp. 37-39.

15

PERSIAN DESIGN CARPET

Herat (eastern Persia) or possibly India, early seventeenth century

SIZE	56 x 78 in.
	(142 x 198 cm.)
WARP	Silk, pale yellow, Z2S, level
WEFT	Cotton, natural, 2–3 shoots after each row of knots
PILE	Wool and some ivory cotton, Persian knot (h. 18, v. 13–15), 234 to 270 knots per square inch
BROCADING	Metallic (gilt and silver on silk core), over 1–under 1; over 3–under 1
SELVEDGES	Overcast, not original
ENDS	Overcast, much repaired
CONDITION	Very fragile, extensively repaired, especially in brocaded areas

Carpets of this design, which have been described as being "as abstract and intricate as a Persian religious discussion"[1] have by common consent been assigned to Herat in eastern Persia, although the possibility of an Indian provenance is argued.[2] This traditional pattern, popular with artists of the sixteenth and seventeenth centuries, features several systems of spiraling vines that spring from the center of the field bearing flowers, buds, and leaves. The tracery is interlaced with graceful cloud bands and a system of large, fan-shaped floral palmettes in a symmetrical "in and out" arrangement. The wide petal edge of the palmettes is brocaded with metallic silver and gilt threads, giving a sumptuous appearance against the rich red wool of the knotted-pile ground. The lobed cartouches that alternate to form the beautiful border contain Chinese cloud bands and quatrefoil lobed devices, skillfully executed at the corners. The guards are undulating vines bearing rosettes and small blossoms.[3]

---

1. Dilley, p. 75.

2. Ellis conjectures (article cited on the next page) that the carpets depicted in European paintings were likely to have been copied from Indian-made carpets of Persian design. Certainly carpets would have been more easily obtainable through the East India trade than from the less accessible Persian sources.

3. The field design, as well as the inner and outer guard bands of this example, may also be seen in Erdmann (1962), pl. 79.

15

PROVENANCE Beshir Galleries, New York
PUBLISHED   Charles Grant Ellis, "Some Compartment Designs for
            Carpets, and Herat," *Textile Museum Journal*, 1 (1965):4,
            fig. 16, pp. 42–56

1963-197

16

PERSIAN CARPET, "VASE" DESIGN
Kerman (southwest Persia), seventeenth century

SIZE	61 x 128 in.
	(155 x 325 cm.)
WARP	Cotton, natural, Z3S, level
WEFT	Cotton (ivory), wool (brown black), 3 shoots of cotton with singles and 2 shoots of black wool at sporadic intervals
PILE	Wool, Persian knot (h. 16, v. 12), about 192 knots per square inch
SELVEDGES	Overcast, faced with heavy linen fabric
ENDS	No apron, short plied cotton fringe (½ in.), faced
CONDITION	Fine, firm weave; reduced in length, some inconspicuous repairs at center top of field

These carpets take their name from flower-filled vases. If included in the field design at all, the vases are subordinate to the profuse display of composite flower palmettes, rosettes, pineapples, and flower sprays compartmented within superimposed lozenges and scalloped medallions. These are arranged symmetrically about the field's vertical axis, a symmetry which is less obvious because of the color variance. A trellis system of light and dark stems, some with forked arabesques and others ornamented with lotus and lily palmettes, form the intricate ground pattern.

Dr. May H. Beattie (see p. xi, Preface) remarks about this example: "A small group of such rugs (late seventeenth century, so-called vase carpets), instead of having floral motifs at the points of juncture of the stems, have lozenge forms with scalloped outlines, pointed ends and floral ornamentation. The Williamsburg rug seems to be a late form of this design

16

which has not been fully understood. The border design is quite usual in Kerman rugs."[1]

PROVENANCE French and Company, New York

1963-729

1. May H. Beattie to John M. Graham II, February 19, 1969, Colonial Williamsburg archives. Erdmann (1962), pl. 74, illustrates an earlier example with which the design of this carpet can be compared.

17

PERSIAN CARPET

Kurdistan (northwest Persia) or Khorassan (eastern Persia),[1] eighteenth century

SIZE	79 x 150 in.
	(198 x 381 cm.)
WARP	Cotton, natural, Z3S, level
WEFT	Cotton, pinkish, 3 shoots after each row
PILE	Wool, Persian (*jūfti*) knot (h. 5½, v. 10), 55 *jūfti* knots per square inch
SELVEDGES	Overcast repairs
ENDS	Cut and repaired at both ends
CONDITION	Worn and repaired, patches in border

Indian influence is noticeable in the coloring and design of this attractive rug with its alternating rows of medallions and floral palmettes with forked arabesques and foliage on the blue floral trellis ground. Because of the popularity of this pattern it may be found in many handsome Caucasian carpets and in less numerous and often fragmentary examples from eastern and northwestern Persia, where the survival rate has not been high because of the poor wearing qualities of the *jūfti* construction, i.e., a practice of knotting on four instead of two warp ends.[2] The wide

1. Ellis suggested to the author that this rug is more likely to be from Kurdistan. The design stems from a seventeenth-century model popular in many areas, and similar designs continue in production to the present day.

2. A large carpet of conventional construction is illustrated in Arts Council of Great Britain, *Islamic Carpets from the Collection of Joseph V. McMullan* (London, 1972), No. 27, pl. 10.

17

palmette border, not uncommon in these rugs, is framed by matching, floral-meander guard bands.

PROVENANCE Arpad Antiques, Washington, D.C.

1968-95

18

PERSIAN CARPET

Kurdistan (northwest Persia), eighteenth or nineteenth century

SIZE	66 x 125 in.
	(168 x 318 cm.)
WARP	Cotton, natural, S3Z, slightly depressed
WEFT	Cotton, natural, S, 2 and 3 shoots
PILE	Wool, Z, Turkish knot (h. 8–9½, v. 10–9½), approximately 90 knots per square inch
SELVEDGES	Overcast, not original
ENDS	Narrow aprons, warp fringe
CONDITION	Some repairs, one end cut and repaired

This rather stiff, geometric example of the flowering tree motif is a late descendant of the garden and paradise carpets.[1] It may be compared with a seventeenth-century example (illustrated in Bode-Kühnel, fig. 101) which is more curvilinear and realistic, but definitely the prototype for this rug with its birds, trees, and flowering shrubs in offset rows.[2] The narrow border is an angular floral meander, with a simple, diagonal-stripe, inner guard.

PROVENANCE Beshir Galleries, New York

1957-175

---

1. May H. Beattie to John M. Graham II, February 19, 1969, Colonial Williamsburg archives.

2. That rug, Ellis notes, and another of similar design in Vienna (Friedrich Sarre and Hermann Trenkwald, *Old Oriental Carpets* [Vienna and London, 1926–1929], vol. 1, pl. 43) were destroyed in World War II. The only surviving example of which he knows is this later one at Williamsburg.

18

Turkish Carpets

TURKEY OR TURKISH carpets were rarely mentioned in colonial records, until the 1740s, when they were occasionally described as "old." After mid-century, however, when imports into western Europe had increased and knotted carpets had become fashionable as floor covering in England, the more affluent colonists adopted the fashion. In August, 1766, John Wayles of Henrico County, Virginia, in a letter to Farrell and Jones, merchants in Bristol, England, comments: "In 1740 I don't remember to have seen such a thing as a turkey Carpet in the Country except a small thing in a bed chamber, Now nothing are so common as Turkey or Wilton Carpetts, the whole Furniture of the Roomes Elegant & every appearance of Opulence."[1]

A typical advertisement in the *Virginia Gazette* of September 5, 1751, listed Turkey carpets among a "Great Variety of fashionable Furniture to be SOLD, for ready Money or short Credit" at Williamsburg. Similar references can be found in merchants' and upholsterers' advertisements in the newspapers of all the large cities. For example, in 1771 "Baker & Yearsley, Silk Dyers & Scowerers from London" advised in the *New York Gazette* and the *Weekly Mercury* that they "clean Turkey and Wilton carpets, and make the colour quite fresh."[2]

Most knotted carpets imported into western Europe in the seventeenth and eighteenth centuries from the Near East, Middle East, and Far East were known as Turkey or Turkish carpets. It can be reasonably assumed, however, that Cairene, Damascus, Persian, Indian, Hispano-Moresque, and possibly some Caucasian products were included under the designation, although very few early records give their exact origin.

The first Oriental carpets quite likely reached Europe with the returning Crusaders, but the primary entrepôt in the sixteenth century was Venice—a port that played an important role in the trade between the Levant and western Europe.

---

1. John M. Hemphill II, ed., "John Wayles Rates His Neighbors," *Virginia Magazine of History and Biography 66* (1958):302–6. John Wayles was Thomas Jefferson's father-in-law. I am indebted to Harold B. Gill for calling this letter to my attention.

2. Rita S. Gottesman, *The Arts and Crafts in New York, 1726–1776* (New York, 1938), p. 285.

Islamic wares of all sorts entered that thriving market, and carpets were among the most important of those wares.[3]

Several carpets at Williamsburg fall into design classifications attributed to the Ushak area of Anatolia, classifications that in recent years have been given names by rug historians and dealers, supposedly in an effort to simplify their identification. Among them, "Lotto" carpets (so called because of their frequent use by the sixteenth-century Italian painter, Lorenzo Lotto) show over-all field patterns of angular arabesques with palmettes and half-palmettes in bright yellow on red or blue grounds, the borders often having interlaced motifs derived from archaic Kufic script (Nos. 19–23). This arabesque design, like those of the somewhat larger star and medallion Ushaks, had as prototypes the more curvilinear Persian designs. A number of Turkish carpets with intricately wrought star motifs alternating with lozenges (Nos. 25–27) have survived from the seventeenth century; their manufacture appears to have ceased by the end of that century. In sharp contrast, the medallion Ushaks (Nos. 28–33) with large central medallion and corner segments on a ground of floral vine tracery—a design that gradually grew more degenerate, coarser, and more rectilinear—continued in popularity and were still being made to order for Europeans in the nineteenth century.

The churches of Transylvania were custodians of large collections of prayer rugs—some with an arabesque field and others having a white ground with so-called bird designs (No. 34). By far the largest group, however, were those of the type illustrated in Nos. 35–37, which have been attributed at various times to the Bergama area of Anatolia, to European Turkey, or to the Transylvania area, where quality rug weaving might well have been carried on under the supervision of the Turkish government. This last group, called "Transylvania church rugs" for want of a more definite provenance, was nevertheless made for export, since the familiar cartouche border designs may be found in several American paintings —Robert Feke's 1741 *Portrait of Isaac Royal and Family*, at the Fogg Art Museum, Harvard University, the *Family Group* by an unknown artist (No. 35A) at Colonial Williamsburg, and others.

Students of these early carpets caution us about linking rug design to dated examples of other decorative arts. However, many of the designs that have become familiar to us through the knotted and flat-woven (*kilim*) carpets of European Turkey and Anatolia may be seen in the tiles and frescoes of Turkey's many mosques, palaces, mausoleums, and churches and in architecture, in jewelry, and quite prominently in the embroideries and pattern-woven silks of the sixteenth

---

3. C. E. C. Tattersall, *A History of British Carpets* (Benfleet, Essex, 1934), pp. 27–28.

and seventeenth centuries. These Islamic designs, showing Chinese, Ottoman, Persian, Syrian, Byzantine, and classical influences, were interpreted by court weavers in very fine rugs of rare beauty and by nomad and village weavers in strong and vibrant colors in coarser constructions.

The knot used in most Turkish carpets is identified as the Turkish or closed knot, or Gördes or Ghiordes knot. Further technical details are included in the caption for each rug.

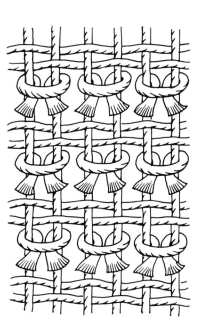

FIGURE 7. *Turkish knot with two shoots of weft*

19

TURKISH CARPET

Anatolia, seventeenth century

SIZE	52 x 76 in.
	(132 x 193 cm.)
WARP	Wool, ivory, ends dipped red, Z2S, alternate warps depressed
WEFT	Wool, dyed red, Z, 2 shoots after each row of knots
PILE	Wool, Turkish knot (h. 6½, v. 8), 52 knots per square inch
SELVEDGES	4 bundles of 2 warp ends wrapped in blue
ENDS	Narrow tabby apron, warp fringe faded light pink
CONDITION	Considerable repairs

In this so-called Lotto arabesque design field with its crudely drawn square "eyes," the pattern is neatly cut off by the border rather than deliberately finished off as was done in the later arabesque carpets such as that shown in No. 21. The angular, halved-lozenge border pattern is not unusual in these rugs, which have been attributed to the Ushak area of Anatolia.

PROVENANCE   Beshir Galleries, New York

1952-143

19

20

TURKISH CARPET

Anatolia, probably seventeenth century

SIZE	45 x 66 in.
	(114 x 168 cm.)
WARP	Wool, ivory, Z2S, slightly depressed
WEFT	Wool, dyed dark red, 2 shoots after each row of knots
PILE	Wool, Turkish knot (h. 7½, v. 9½), approximately 71 knots per square inch
SELVEDGES	3 bundles of 2 warp ends, wrapped in brown, repairs
ENDS	Cut and repaired, lower end rewoven
CONDITION	Medium quality, considerable abrasion and repairs

The field pattern of angular arabesques terminates in full and half palmettes forming various geometric devices. The angular ribbon work of the main border is derived from archaic Kufic lettering and is strictly decorative. The outer guard band has small leaves arranged to form rosettes. The unusually clear ivory, the dark red of the field, and the abraded surface have raised questions as to whether this rug was not made later than the seventeenth century.

PROVENANCE   Beshir Galleries, New York

1952-141

20

21

TURKISH CARPET

Anatolia, late seventeenth century or later

Size	63 x 105 in. (161 x 266 cm.)
Warp	Wool, ivory, Z2S, depressed
Weft	Wool, red, 2 shoots after each row of knots
Pile	Wool, Turkish knot (h. 8, v. 10), 80 knots per square inch
Selvedges	Repaired, not original
Ends	Narrow apron with warp fringe
Condition	Fine weave, rewoven at lower end

This carpet has been referred to as "A Turkish Rug showing the 'Lotto Pattern' in the Transylvanian Manner," suggesting that this particular example was made in the Ushak area of Anatolia, having been copied from a Transylvanian church carpet that had probably been produced in a manufactory in European Turkey.[1]

Compared with the more curvilinear arabesques in the field of No. 20, the rather stiffly spiked and stepped drawing of this particular example is suggestive of *kilim* (tapestry-woven) rugs. The reciprocal palmette border occurs with various field patterns in surviving Anatolian carpets. However, the outer guard band is not typical and further study may determine that this carpet is indeed a later copy. The extremely good condition also tends to belie the earlier dating.

PROVENANCE Beshir Galleries, New York

1952-140

---

1. Ellis, p. 53

21

22

TURKISH CARPET

Probably Anatolia, early eighteenth century

SIZE	52 x 69 in.
	(132 x 175 cm.)
WARP	Wool, ivory, Z2S, slightly depressed
WEFT	Wool, red, 2 shoots after each row of knots
PILE	Wool, Turkish knot (h. 8, v. 10), 80 knots per square inch
SELVEDGES	Overcast, not original
ENDS	No apron, ragged warp fringe
CONDITION	Considerable repairs (rebuilding)

As discussed in No. 21, this is another of the carpets probably made in the Ushak area of Anatolia, having been copied from earlier examples found in considerable numbers in the churches of Transylvania, which at that time was under Turkish rule. In this example, the field pattern lacks the crispness usually found in the Transylvanian rugs, but the small stars and other geometric motifs incorporated in the arabesque field are characteristic. The border pattern of cloud bands alternating with rosettes is often associated with this field design, as well as with the so-called bird carpets of the seventeenth century (see No. 34).

PROVENANCE   Beshir Galleries, New York

1956-174

22

23

TURKISH CARPET

Anatolia, eighteenth or nineteenth century

SIZE	45 x 72 in.
	(119 x 183 cm.)
WARP	Wool, ivory, Z2S, only very slightly depressed
WEFT	Wool, red, 2 shoots after each row of knots
PILE	Wool, Turkish knot (h. 9½, v. 10), 95 to 100 knots per square inch
SELVEDGES	5 bundles of 2, light green tabby
ENDS	Narrow red tabby apron, short warp fringe
CONDITION	Fine, even weave, some reknotting of outlines

Although this carpet design is similar to other arabesque rugs in the collection, several relevant features are worth mentioning. The outer guard, as well as the main border, is similar to those appearing in paintings by Lorenzo Lotto, although the inner guard and the treatment of the field design along the edges of the border appear to be later. Furthermore, the large number of well-preserved rugs of this type extant in Europe and America, although not made of synthetically dyed wools, lead carpet specialists to question whether they might be eighteenth or even nineteenth, rather than seventeenth century. It is generally felt that much more study is required, especially in view of the opinion expressed by Erdmann that "degeneration of design, so frequent in late examples of other groups, hardly ever occurs. . . . Apparently the Lotto carpets disappeared as suddenly at the end of the seventeenth century as they had appeared at the beginning of the sixteenth. There is no evidence that even some of their designs survived into the eighteenth and nineteenth centuries. It is as if the workshops which had produced them had suddenly closed their doors or had started to make carpets of a different kind."[1]

PROVENANCE   Beshir Galleries, New York

1954-648

---

1. Erdmann (1970), p. 60.

23

24

TURKISH "PRAYER" CARPET
Anatolia, probably eighteenth century

SIZE	45 x 65 in.
	(114 x 165 cm.)
WARP	Wool, tan, Z2S, depressed, ends dipped red
WEFT	Wool, red, Z, 2 shoots, diagonals
PILE	Wool, Turkish knot (h. 10, v. 11½), 115 knots per square inch
SELVEDGES	Overcast, not original
ENDS	Cut and overcast
CONDITION	Several mended areas, dark greenish-black areas of spandrels eroded

Certainly produced in the Ushak area of western Anatolia, rugs such as this with opposed niches were not among the types most sought by Europeans, and few were exported.[1] The central motif is a hexagonal medallion with quatrefoil center. Lacy scrollwork with half palmettes and other floral devices form the spandrels that define the niches at each end of the field. A decorative pendant hangs from the apex of one arch. The wide border of floral scrolls and stylized lotus palmettes interlaced with arabesques is typical of these rugs. The guards, however, appear to be stiff, misunderstood versions of the lotus-trail pattern commonly used in earlier rugs. A good example of this border is depicted by Mathieu LeNain (Laon, 1607–Paris, 1677) in *The Backgammon Players*, in the Louvre.[2]

PROVENANCE   Beshir Galleries, New York

1957-128

---

1. Erdmann (1970), p. 155.

2. Illustrated in *French Paintings from French Museums* (San Diego, 1967). Maurice S. Dimand, *The Ballard Collection of Oriental Rugs* (St. Louis, 1935), pl. 19, and Erdmann (1962), fig. 145, show rugs of similar field and border design. Other examples are in the collection of the Philadelphia Museum of Art (43–40–60 and 55–65–17), according to Ellis, who is presently engaged in writing a catalog of that collection.

24

25

TURKISH CARPET

Anatolia (possibly Ushak), seventeenth century

SIZE	77 x 138 in.
	(196 x 351 cm.)
WARP	Wool, ivory, Z2S, slightly depressed
WEFT	Wool, red, 2 shoots, some diagonals
PILE	Wool, Turkish knot (h. 6½, v. 9), 58 knots per square inch
SELVEDGES	Overcast, not original
ENDS	Repaired
CONDITION	Medium quality, repairs in field and border

Carpets like this appear in sixteenth- and seventeenth-century paintings, and their color scheme is even more stereotyped than that of the related carpets—with large center medallions—which are also attributed to the Ushak area.[1] Large arabesque-filled, eight-pointed stars of intricate form alternate, in all directions, with smaller lozenge medallions of similar infloriation on a floral groundwork of palmettes, rosettes, foliage, and stem tracery. The bicolored border in reciprocal outline is uncommon in Anatolian carpets, although an early star Ushak with similar border is illustrated in Bode-Kühnel, fig. 22.[2]

PROVENANCE   Beshir Galleries, New York

1958-636

---

1. Bode-Kühnel, pp. 42–45.
2. Two other rugs with this uncommon type of border in the Philadelphia Museum (43-40-66 and 55-65-16) have been called to my attention by Charles Grant Ellis.

25

26

26A
"Edmund, 3rd Baron Sheffield,
1st Earl of Mulgrave," oil,
Flemish, painted by Van Somer,
dated 1614, showing a portion of
a star medallion carpet. Colonial
Williamsburg Foundation,
G1941-259.

26

TURKISH CARPET

Anatolia (Ushak),
seventeenth century

SIZE	54 x 116 in.
	(137 x 195 cm.)
WARP	Wool, ivory, Z3S, alternate warps depressed
WEFT	Wool and mixed fiber, tan and light red, 2 shoots
PILE	Wool, Turkish knot (h. 7, v. 9), 63 knots per square inch
SELVEDGES	Overcast, not original
ENDS	Repairs
CONDITION	Considerable reweaving at both ends, outer guards appear to be replacements

The two star and lozenge medallions in offset rows show a more symmetrically arranged field than that of No. 25. An undulating vine partitions the border, in which flower palmettes alternate with candelabra-like motifs, a border found in other examples and depicted in paintings. Colonial Williamsburg owns a portrait (see No. 26A) of Edmund, third baron Sheffield, first earl of Mulgrave, dated 1614 and painted by the Flemish painter Van Somer, that shows the baron standing on a carpet in which part of a star medallion is clearly visible in the lower left foreground.

PROVENANCE Beshir Galleries, New York

1954-58

27

TURKISH CARPET

Anatolia (Ushak), probably seventeenth century

SIZE	63 x 94 in.
	(161 x 239 cm.)
WARP	Wool, ivory, Z2S, alternate warps depressed
WEFT	Wool, red, Z, 2 shoots after each row of knots
PILE	Wool, Turkish knot (h. 8, v. 12½), about 100 knots per square inch
SELVEDGES	4 bundles of 2 ends each, tabby
ENDS	Worn, overcast
CONDITION	Fine weave, considerable reknotting

Two rather compressed eight-pointed stars linked to lozenges are super-imposed on a ground pattern of floral scrolls and vine tracery character-istic of this type of carpet. The border, showing a "marked retroverted hook" and vine bearing "crumpled arabesque leaf" has been noted in only one other rug—a star Ushak in the Black Church in Brașov, Romania. It is impossible, at present, to determine whether or not this is a skillful copy of the Brașov carpet. We may perhaps allow this fine example the benefit of the doubt.[1] It may be compared with No. 26, which has a simi-lar field but a different border.

PROVENANCE   Beshir Galleries, New York

1953-537

---

1. May H. Beattie to John M. Graham II, February 29, 1969, Colonial Williamsburg archives.

27

28

TURKISH CARPET

Anatolia (Ushak), seventeenth or eighteenth century

SIZE	84 x 154 in.
	(239 x 391 cm.)
WARP	Wool, ivory, Z2S, alternate warps depressed
WEFT	Wool, dyed red, Z, 2 shoots after each row of knots
PILE	Wool, Turkish knot (h. 7, v. 9), 63 knots per square inch
SELVEDGES	4 bundles of 2 ends each, tabby
ENDS	No apron or fringe
CONDITION	Ends and sides restored, left border guard a replacement of a different pattern

A comparison with No. 29 will indicate how compressed—depleted of design elements—this center medallion is. The large arabesques, the leaf forms, and the vertically placed palmettes have all been omitted. The usual deeply indented outer fringelike trim prominent in most examples is here virtually obliterated, leaving the narrow serrate edge in outline around the central shield and considerably altering the field design. There are lozenge pendants on the vertical axis (somewhat distorted by repairs), and indented medallion segments form corner motifs on the floral-trail ground. The wide border shows a variety of floral palmettes interspersed with trailing stems bearing blossoms and foliage.

PROVENANCE   Beshir Galleries, New York

1953-538

28

29

TURKISH CARPET

Anatolia (Ushak), seventeenth or eighteenth century

SIZE	92 x 144 in.
	(234 x 366 cm.)
WARP	Wool, ivory, Z2S, alternate warps depressed
WEFT	Wool, dyed red, Z, 2 shoots after each row of knots
PILE	Wool, Turkish knot (h. 7, v. 9), 63 knots per square inch
SELVEDGES	Not original, overcast
ENDS	Worn, no apron, mixed fiber pulled in to form fringe
CONDITION	Repaired at top and bottom, guards missing at both ends

Although somewhat compressed, the large hexagonal medallion makes an interesting comparison with No. 32. While sizes and proportions of rugs in this group varied, the typical technique, color scheme, and basic design elements remained constant throughout the long period of manufacture. In this carpet the quatrefoil center of the large medallion, with its arabesques, palmettes, and half-palmettes, as well as the pendant medallions and the indented corner sections are more clearly and carefully delineated than in the later examples. The border with a repeat motif of composite floral palmettes is not one of the most common; however, there appear to be several other medallion Ushaks in American collections in which similar border designs are to be found.[1]

PROVENANCE   Beshir Galleries, New York

1959-109

---

1. May H. Beattie to John M. Graham II, February 29, 1969, Colonial Williamsburg archives.

29

30

TURKISH CARPET

Anatolia (Ushak), eighteenth or nineteenth century

SIZE	129 x 234 in.
	(328 x 594 cm.)
WARP	Wool, ivory, ends dipped red, Z2S, depressed
WEFT	Wool, reddish, Z singles and Z2S, 2 and 3 shoots and diagonals
PILE	Wool, Turkish knot (h. 5, v. 5–5½), 25 to 28 knots per square inch
SELVEDGES	4 cord tabby
ENDS	Worn and repaired
CONDITION	Coarse quality, considerable repairs to field and borders at both ends, outer guard at bottom replaced

This large carpet of traditional design now designated as a "medallion Ushak" differs from No. 29, of earlier date, in that it is very much coarser and shows the disintegration of the scrolling floral vine into a small, repetitive floral device. This diapered-effect ground patterning continued in use in the "Smyrna" carpets that were produced throughout the nineteenth century in Europe as well as in Turkey (see No. 31).

PROVENANCE Beshir Galleries, New York

1937-271

30

31

TURKISH CARPET

Anatolia or Europe, nineteenth century

SIZE	103 x 173 in.
	(262 x 438 cm.)
WARP	Wool, tan-brown interplied (barber pole), ends dipped red, Z2S, alternate warps depressed
WEFT	Wool, dyed red, Z, 2 shoots and some diagonals
PILE	Wool, Turkish knot (h. 4½–5, v. 6½–8), 36 to 40 knots per square inch
SELVEDGES	Overcast, not original
ENDS	Top repaired, lower end rewoven
CONDITION	Coarse and firm, considerable repairs

The large hexagonal center medallion is compartmented by crossed arabesques and filled, as are the pendant cartouches and deeply indented spandrels, with stylized floral and vine tracery. The rather strangely drawn border has alternating floral palmettes. Such carpets, not very individualistic in design (see Nos. 28 and 32), were made in great numbers in the vicinity of Ushak, an area east of Smyrna. The latter was an important seaport of Asia Minor around which the carpet trade flourished. These well-proportioned carpets, often manufactured under direct European control, were in great demand throughout the eighteenth century. Large commissions for them came from Holland, England, and other European countries. Carpets of this traditional medallion design were also produced, some by hand and some on the newly mechanized carpet looms, in several European countries during the nineteenth century, which complicates identification.[1]

PROVENANCE Beshir Galleries, New York

1952-139

---

1. A. Varron, "The Beginnings of the Modern Carpet Industry," *Ciba Review, The European Carpet,* No. 23 (Basle, July 1939), pp. 816–20. Of this European carpet manufacture Varron remarks: "Whereas in the 17th and 18th centuries, the Oriental motifs were transformed and adapted until they became new and independent designs [see Nos. 3 and 5], the 19th century with its unproductive imitation of past styles merely copied the Oriental designs. In 1856 the first so-called Smyrna carpets were made at Schmiedeberg (Silesia) in Germany. . . ."

31

32

TURKISH CARPET

Anatolia (Ushak-Smyrna district),
eighteenth or nineteenth century

SIZE	72 x 120 in.
	(183 x 305 cm.)
WARP	Wool, yellowish, ends dipped red, Z2S, alternate warps depressed
WEFT	Wool, dyed dark red, Z, 2 shoots, some diagonals
PILE	Wool, Turkish knot (h. 7, v. 8), 56 knots per square inch
SELVEDGES	Overcast, not original
ENDS	Repaired, mixed-fiber fringe added
CONDITION	Coarse weave, some of the repairs have been made with cotton (pile)

A number of these so-called medallion Ushaks of disputed date are illustrated here in order that design, color, and quality comparisons may be made. The misinterpretation of traditional design elements shows in the diminished and much-distorted angularity of the center medallion with its degenerate arabesques and in the nondescript corner motifs. The traditional floral tracery of the field is easily recognizable, but the harsh blues and the sculptured rendition, as can be seen here, are sometimes found in the late carpets of this design group.

PROVENANCE   Beshir Galleries, New York

1958-261

32

33

33

TURKISH "MEDALLION" CARPET
Anatolia (Ushak), undetermined date

SIZE	120 x 236 in.
	(305 x 599 cm.)
WARP	Wool, ivory, ends dipped red, Z2S, depressed
WEFT	Wool, dark red, Z, 2 shoots
PILE	Wool, Turkish knot (h. 8, v. 11), 88 knots per square inch
	(abrash in lower portion of center)
SELVEDGES	Overcast, not original
ENDS	Repaired
CONDITION	Fine even weave, considerable repair to worn areas, including some reknotting of center medallion. No wear appears deliberate, as in a forgery

Of the six specialists who have examined this carpet or a true color transparency of it during the twenty years it has been owned by Colonial Williamsburg, three have expressed the opinion that it was a fine and rare Ushak, probably seventeenth century. The other three expressed doubts about such lavish use of pinks and greens in seventeenth- and eighteenth-century carpets and suggested that the colors be tested to determine if chemical dyes were used. This was thought advisable and comparative analysis, including chromatography, was recently performed.[1] The results of comparative tests between pile-wool (blues, green, and pink) from this example and the same colors extracted from the original portions of a documented seventeenth-century Ushak[2] confirmed that this carpet, of con-

---

1. Courtesy of the color and dye-testing laboratory of the E. I. du Pont de Nemours Company, Wilmington, Delaware.

2. Carpet 1938-49, too worn to include in this catalog. Also included in this test were examples of the same colors extracted from late nineteenth- or early twentieth-century Iranian rugs which, because of their aniline content, provided comparative material for the physical (ultraviolet and spectrophotometric) and chemical (thin layer chromatography) examination of 1953-571.

siderably finer construction than the later Ushaks, was not an aniline-dyed production.

"This is the type of handsome medallion Ushak design which one usually associates with early examples, and which is portrayed in the *Allegory of the Peaceful Reign of Queen Elizabeth* attributed to Hans Eworth, ca. 1565–70. This is the first known occurrence of the design in Western painting."[3] The pattern, whose prototype was the classical Persian medallion carpet, is related stylistically to the sixteenth-century Anatolian carpets often illustrated,[4] its primary and questionable difference being the extensive use of pinks and greens in the central medallion. This deviation from the normal is not entirely without precedent however, since Erdmann illustrates fragments of a similar carpet of the sixteenth century in which the medallion on the central axis has a light yellow ground. Since all of the more than one thousand examples known to him prior to this discovery employed the traditional coloring (red field), he found it sufficiently interesting to acquire for the Islamic Department, Berlin State Museums, noting that it presumably was "a unique but not quite successful experimental piece. . . ."[5]

Questions still to be answered are: Is the Williamsburg example such an experimental piece? Is it a late and rather ambitious reproduction of this early design group, made in the eighteenth century? Or is it a late nineteenth-century production from a manufactory which had continued to use natural dyes? As to the last question, Beattie states: "From literary sources I know that green was extremely popular in Turkish rugs in the mid-nineteenth century, and the later copying of an early design combined with a current vogue for green might well explain this rug."[6]

PROVENANCE   Beshir Galleries, New York

1953-571

3. May H. Beattie to John M. Graham II, February 19, 1969, Colonial Williamsburg archives.

4. Ignace Schlosser, *The Book of Rugs* (New York, 1963), fig. 10; Dilley, pl. LXI (right), and Bode-Kühnel, fig. 20.

5. Erdmann (1970), pp. 158–59.

6. See note 3 above.

34

"BIRD" CARPET

> Possibly Transylvania or European Turkey,[1] original part (less than one half of carpet) probably seventeenth century

SIZE	46 x 66 in.
	(117 x 168 cm.)
WARP	Wool, ivory, Z2S, slightly depressed
WEFT	Wool, yellowish, Z, 2 shoots and diagonals (repairs?)
PILE	Wool, 2 qualities Z-spun, Turkish knot (h. 8, v. 8–9), 64 to 72 knots per square inch
CONDITION	Approximately 60 percent reknotted, ends and selvedges replaced, cotton or mixed-fiber fringe added

This design, its birdlike abstract leaves alternating vertically and laterally with misunderstood flower palmettes, forms rectangles containing rosette-lily motifs. When a comparison is made with less-repaired examples,[2] discrepancies show in the cartoon-drafted, repetitive design of the field. The bird palmette is ill formed and cut off along the border at the sides, and the geometric form (alternating with "birds" on the central axis) appears in other rugs as a floral rosette around which the "birds" radiate in pinwheel fashion. The cloud-band motif in the border, which like many other designs in early rugs stems from Chinese symbolism,

---

1. Ellis, p. 53, says of these rugs: "The origin of these Transylvanian rugs remains a puzzle. . . . Probably the manufacture was in European Turkey, possibly somewhere in Thrace. Attempts to ascribe these rugs to a variety of centers in Anatolia are not convincing, particularly to one who has seen many of the pieces themselves."

2. Bode-Kühnel, pp. 51–53, figs. 29, 31, 32 (border designs). This border's Persian prototype is beautifully illustrated in Erdmann (1970), p. 83, fig. 229, a Tabriz animal carpet of the sixteenth century. For the field design, cf. Erdmann (1970), p. 206, fig. 263; Erdmann (1962), fig. 148; *Islamic Carpets in the Collection of Joseph V. McMullan* (London: The Arts Council of Great Britain, 1972), pl. XXVI, p. 76.

34

alternates on three sides with large rosettes—on the lower edge with stylized carnations, both on angular stems intersected by cruciform motifs. Such rugs are still to be found in the churches of Transylvania, and since they are among the older pieces, they are often so worn that the original pattern is difficult to discern. Laws have been enacted to prevent the removal of the old rugs from these churches. However, in the early twentieth century, when they were available, many worn examples were purchased and very skillfully, if sometimes erroneously, repaired or even reconstructed by the adept carpet weavers of eastern Europe. Some of these reconstructed rugs are still to be seen in Romania and elsewhere. This carpet may be one of these, since the original parts are probably seventeenth century.[3]

PROVENANCE   Beshir Galleries, New York

1957-38

3. May H. Beattie to John M. Graham II, February 29, 1969, Colonial Williamsburg archives.

34 A
Detail of upper right of No. 34 showing areas where reknotting is discernible.

35

35

TURKISH "TRANSYLVANIA CHURCH" CARPET
Seventeenth or eighteenth century

SIZE	49 x 62 in.
	(124 x 157 cm.)
WARP	Wool, ivory, ends dipped yellow-green, Z2S, alternate warps slightly depressed
WEFT	Wool, dyed red, Z, 2 shoots, some irregularities
PILE	Wool, Z, Turkish knot (h. 7½, v. 8), 60 knots per square inch
SELVEDGES	3 bundles of 2 wrapped with olive green wool
ENDS	Tabby-woven aprons of olive green wool, cut fringe upper end, worn looped fringe at lower end
CONDITION	Good condition, some skillful repairs

The symmetrically opposed niches and the oblong cartouches, sometimes alternating with eight-pointed stars, make rugs of this type the most easily identifiable of the so-called Transylvania prayer or church rugs. In this example, border guards of rosettes replace the usual reciprocal trefoil (lily) guards. It has been suggested that the term "prayer rug" can be reasonably applied to pieces with opposed niche designs, but classification is simplified if the unqualified term is restricted to the asymmetrical design. The *mirab*, or niche, an architectural term adapted from the mosque, was not necessarily a requisite feature of a prayer rug, since any carpet devoid of animal design might provide the "clean place" on which the Moslem was enjoined to pray.[1] As was the custom in the eighteenth century, this example is used as a covering on a table, now in the large upper middle room of the Governor's Palace in Williamsburg. A number of carpets of the type appear in English and American paintings of the eighteenth century,[2] and one by an unknown art-

---

1. May H. Beattie, *The Rug in Islamic Art*, catalog of an exhibition held at Temple Newsam House (Leeds, 1964), no. 11.

2. *Portrait of Isaac Royall and Family* by Robert Feke, 1741 (Harvard University, Fogg Art Museum), depicts a table carpet of very much the same pattern as No. 35.

35A
*"Family Group," oil, artist
unknown. Colonial Williamsburg
Foundation, 1939-247.*

ist (No. 35A), once believed to be of the prominent John Blair family of
Williamsburg, is reproduced here.

PROVENANCE   Beshir Galleries, New York

1954-57

36

TURKISH "TRANSYLVANIA CHURCH" CARPET

Seventeenth or eighteenth century

SIZE	46 x 63 in. (117 x 160 cm.)
WARP	Wool, tan (yellowish), some tan-brown interplied barber pole, Z2S, alternate warps depressed
WEFT	Wool, dyed light red, Z, 2 shoots after row of knots
PILE	Wool, Z, Turkish knot (h. 9, v. 9½), 86 knots per square inch
SELVEDGES	Repaired, overcast
ENDS	No aprons, worn warp-end fringes dipped yellowish-tan
CONDITION	Fine, firm weave, minor repairs

"Lamps" or "vases" hang in the apex of the niches at either end of the
field of this prayer rug, which is symmetrically arranged from side to side

36

but not from end to end. An atypical rosette form used in the spandrels and the introduction of a bright blue motif at regular intervals in the reciprocal trefoil guard at one end are unusual elements in this example. Many of the design features of this carpet—the outline pattern of the central field, the similar vase and palmette treatment, as well as the border cartouches and reciprocal guards—are similar in draftsmanship in the later carpet illustrated as No. 42.

PROVENANCE   Beshir Galleries, New York
PUBLISHED   Ellis, p. 51

1956-252

37

TURKISH CARPET

Possibly a nineteenth-century copy of a "Transylvanian church" rug made in Anatolia

SIZE	48 x 72 in.
	(122 x 183 cm.)
WARP	Wool, ivory with ends dipped red, Z2S, depressed
WEFT	Wool, pink (apron weft, olive green), Z, 2 shoots
PILE	Wool, Turkish knot (h. 10, v. 9½–10), 95 to 100 knots per square inch
SELVEDGES	4 bundles, 2 cords each olive green
ENDS	Aprons tabby-weave, olive green weft, red warp-end fringe (short and ragged)
CONDITION	Fine, firm weave with deep, clean pile

As previously stated, considerable numbers of carpets woven in various parts of Turkey in traditional designs found their way into churches of the Transylvania region, now a part of Romania, and carpets of traditional patterns—copies of these church rugs—continued to be made somewhere in this region well into the nineteenth century. The unusually silky pile, even weave, clear, bright colors, and pristine condition of this example suggest that it might be of that category—an early nineteenth-century copy of a traditional pattern.

37

The provenance of the so-called Transylvanian church carpets is still questionable, but European Turkey, of which this Balkan area was once a part, is one of the possibilities. Ellis has pointed out that apparently many rugs were brought to Anatolia by returning bureaucrats and copied there, producing new local varieties in the Bergama and Konia areas.[1]

PROVENANCE   Beshir Galleries, New York

1956-146

---

1. Ellis, p. 53.

Caucasian Carpets

BRIGHT COLORS and bold geometric patterning, usually darker wool warp and weft, and somewhat deeper wool pile characterized the eighteenth-century carpets woven in the Caucasus—an austere and remote region lying between the Black and the Caspian Seas and divided in area by the formidable Caucasian Mountains. The sparse and rebellious population resisted conquering forces until the mid-nineteenth century when Russia finally established territorial rule and, subsequently, commerce with the western world.

The carpets from this region reflect the culture of many races and religions —Armenians, Turks, Persians, Mongols, Kurds, and Tatars—many of whom were nomadic tribes. Each made contributions to the designs of various groups, and "strange as the design undertaken may be, the outcome of the amalgamation is always a typical Caucasian solution. . . . It is as if the unfamiliar forms were plunged into a bath from which they emerge again in Caucasian styling."[1]

Represented in the collection at Williamsburg are several so-called dragon rugs of the eighteenth century, and others compartmented by long serrate leaves enclosing floral palmettes and treelike motifs which, even in their severe angularity, show their relation to Persian prototypes. This range of examples, generally ascribed to the Kuba district, an important center on the Caspian coast, also illustrates the transition of the dragon and other animal and bird forms into the unrecognizable plantlike motifs they were to become by the early eighteenth century.

---

1. Erdmann (1962), p. 46.

38

CAUCASIAN "DRAGON" CARPET

Kuba, early eighteenth century

SIZE	98 x 150 in. (249 x 381 cm.)
WARP	Wool, tan-brown barber pole, Z2S, alternate warps depressed
WEFT	Wool, dyed pink, Z, 2 shoots and singles
PILE	Wool, Turkish knot (h. 9, v. 7–8½), 63 to 75 knots per square inch
SELVEDGES	Overcast, not original
ENDS	Repaired, mixed-fiber fringes pulled in
CONDITION	Very much rebuilt in lower central area and upper corners, reduced in length

Two pairs of confronting, rather degenerate, dragons and other almost unrecognizable animal and bird forms are depicted, with elongated leaves enclosing leafy palmettes in trellised compartments. While not rare in dragon rugs, the blue ground is more unusual than red and the palmette border is more often associated with vine-leaf and other patterns on blue grounds (see Nos. 42 and 43). The rather cut-off design at the lower end of the field leads one to surmise that the rug has been shortened, and close examination reveals a very neat join across the lower third of the rug. Charles Ellis believes that the rug had a uniquely different design with probably another pair of dragons below, like those in the upper register. Possibly the entire upper register had at one time been duplicated at the bottom of the rug. These alterations had been made before Pope illustrated it in 1922.[1]

PROVENANCE Beshir Galleries, New York

1952-138

---

1. Arthur U. Pope, "Oriental Rugs as Fine Art," *International Studio* 76 (November 1922):167.

38

39

39 A
Detail of dragon

39

CAUCASIAN "DRAGON" CARPET

Kuba, eighteenth century

SIZE	84 x 181 in.
	(213 x 458 cm.)
WARP	Wool, tan and barber pole, Z2S,
	alternate warps depressed
WEFT	Wool, dyed red, Z, 2 shoots, singles,
	some diagonals
PILE	Wool, Turkish knot (h. 7½–8, v. 8–9), 60 to 72 knots per square
	inch
SELVEDGES	Overcast, repairs
ENDS	Repairs, mixed-fiber fringe ends added
CONDITION	Good, some well-executed repairs

Prominent in the field are pairs of severely stylized dragons in confronting and addorsed positions, arranged symmetrically on the field's vertical axis. The dragons (one pair cut in half) are compartmented by elongated light- and dark-ground serrate leaves arranged lattice fashion, each leaf being ornamented with an angular flowering vine. Guard bands with reciprocally arranged trefoils frame the simple, narrow border of flower-enclosed hexagons.

This carpet is one of a large group, many with blue and blue-green grounds with varying degrees of inversion of elements (seen here in the ivory leaf forms) and all with degenerate dragons. In this class the content of the lower register moves sideways for half its width in each successive register up the pattern. Thus dragons change direction at each level, and forms that are on the center line of one register are on the side axis of the next.[1] Examples can be found at the Türk

---

1. I am indebted to Charles Ellis for this descriptive information.

ve Islam Museum in Istanbul, the Philadelphia Museum of Art, the Textile Museum in Washington, D.C., and the Ima Hogg Collection at Bayou Bend, Houston, Texas.

PROVENANCE   Beshir Galleries, New York

1963-198

40

CAUCASIAN "DRAGON" CARPET

Kuba, eighteenth century

SIZE   75 x 98 in.
             (191 x 249 cm.)
WARP   Wool, tan and barber pole, Z2S, depressed
WEFT   Wool, reddish, Z, 2 shoots and singles
PILE   Wool, Z, Turkish knot (h. 8, v. 8-9), 64 to 72 knots per square inch
SELVEDGES   Overcast, not original
ENDS   Worn, ragged warp fringe on attached border ends
CONDITION   Firm weave, a fragment of a larger rug

The colors are bright and pleasing in this piece, which is probably the lower left section cut from a much larger carpet, as indicated by the size of the large spikey palmettes and the one degenerate dragon positioned slightly left of center. On the right edge of the field it is possible to see that the dragon and other elements begin to repeat mirror-wise in the lower registers; the top right palmette and other motifs have been somewhat distorted by patches. The over-all design as it might have appeared before the reduction in size can be seen in a carpet at Dumbarton Oaks.[1]

PROVENANCE   Beshir Galleries, New York
PUBLISHED   F. Lewis, *Oriental Rugs and Textiles, The Perez Collection* (London, 1953), p. 7, pl. 37

1954-59

———
1. Catalog of the Textile Museum, *Exhibition of Dragon Rugs* (Washington, D.C., 1948), frontispiece.

40

41

CAUCASIAN "DRAGON" CARPET
Kuba, late eighteenth century

SIZE	90 x 141 in.
	(229 x 358 cm.)
WARP	Wool, tan and barber pole, Z2S, depressed
WEFT	Wool, light red, Z, 2 shoots and singles
PILE	Wool, Turkish knot (h. 8–9, v. 7½–9), 60 to 81 knots per square inch
SELVEDGES	Overcast, not original
ENDS	Cut and repaired
CONDITION	Somewhat reduced in length, repaired

In this late example the two pairs of degenerate dragons and several of the highly stylized leaf and palmette forms are reversed in side-to-side and rather clumsy end-to-end mirror image, instead of the drop-repeat arrangement common to these carpets. Ellis and Beattie pointed out in discussions with the writer that a number of these dragon rugs show efforts at a balanced design through inversion of areas or elements. Another pair of dragons probably appeared toward the lower end before the carpet was reduced in length.

Related rugs of twofold lattice design with degenerate dragons and no other animal or bird forms are to be found in the Türk ve Islam Museum in Istanbul; one formerly at the Staatliche Museen, Berlin, was destroyed by fire in 1945.[1]

PROVENANCE   Beshir Galleries, New York

1959-108

---

1. Ignace Schlosser, *The Book of Rugs, Oriental and European* (New York, 1960), fig. 76, and Erdmann (1962), pl. 98, show the Berlin example.

41

42

CAUCASIAN CARPET

Kuba, eighteenth century

SIZE	92 x 146 in.
	(234 x 371 cm.)
WARP	Wool, natural, Z2S, depressed
WEFT.	Wool, pink, Z, 2 shoots and fat singles, Z3S
PILE	Wool, Z, Turkish knot (h. 8–10, v. 9–11), 72 to 110 knots per square inch
SELVEDGES	Overcast, repairs
ENDS	Mixed-fiber tabby aprons with fringe
CONDITION	Reduced in length, lower third finer construction than upper portion

Characteristic of this group of carpets, some of which are extremely handsome, are the blue-green ground and the rows of lily palmettes flanked by large serrate leaves which alternate horizontally and in offset rows with large vine-leaf palmettes whose vertical axes lie laterally in the field. Smaller palmettes, rosettes, and leaves cover the intervening spaces. The border of geometric floral meander is often found in carpets of this type. A portion of this rug, on close examination, appears to be from another carpet of finer construction which has been adroitly joined across the lower third of the field.

PROVENANCE   Beshir Galleries, New York

1954-60

42

43

CAUCASIAN CARPET

Kuba, eighteenth century

SIZE	95 x 202 in.
	(241 x 513 cm.)
WARP	Wool, tan and some barber pole, Z2S, depressed
WEFT	Wool, reddish interplied with tan cotton, Z2S3Z, 2 shoots and fat singles
PILE	Wool, Z, Turkish knot (h. 7, v. 8–8½), 56 to 60 knots per square inch
SELVEDGES	Overcast, not original
ENDS	Repaired, mixed-fiber fringe added
CONDITION	Coarse weave, considerable repairs

The center and outer rows of the field are composed of stylized lily palmettes with angular stems terminating in large sickle leaves. Arranged on the vertical axis, laterally "in and out," are pairs of large, ornamented floral and leaf palmettes. The unbalanced color scheme in rugs of this class tends to distort the symmetry of the pattern, which in this example is mirror image whereas in No. 42 it is only from side to side, probably due to the reduction in length. The border and guards of types usual in these rugs include running vine and trefoils enclosing the wider floral meander.

PROVENANCE   Gift of Mrs. Robert McKay, Long Island, New York

G1963-733

43

44

CAUCASIAN CARPET

Kuba, first half of the eighteenth century

SIZE	92 x 183 in.
	(234 x 465 cm.)
WARP	Wool, tan and barber pole, Z2S, alternate warps depressed
WEFT	Wool, light red, Z, 2 shoots and fat singles
PILE	Wool, Z, Turkish knot (h. 8, v. 8–9), 64 to 72 knots per square inch
SELVEDGES	2 bundles, 2 ends, repaired
ENDS	Cut and repaired, lower end a replacement
CONDITION	Medium firm weave, strip 2–5 inches wide inset (left of center) the entire length of carpet, probably reduced in length and width

This splendid rug is one of a group of Caucasian carpets that has long been associated with the area around Kuba. The design, which clearly derives from Persian art, has elongated infoliate leaves which do not interlace lattice fashion, as in the dragon rugs to which this example is related. Instead, they spring symmetrically from three-lobed, palmette-filled medallions to form ogival compartments on the vertical line, framing palmettes which have become elongated into cypress trees. The outer rows show cypress palmettes growing vertically along the border in the opposite direction, and alternating with serrate-edge hexagons. The ground is interspersed with a system of angular stems bearing blossoms and foliage. Reciprocal trefoil guard bands enclose a narrow border of leaf palmettes alternating with stylized trees. A variant of this cypress tree motif appears in a Caucasian carpet fragment in the collections of the Türk ve Islam Museum in Istanbul.[1]

PROVENANCE French and Company, New York

1963-199

---

1. Erdmann (1970), p. 111, fig. 131.

44

45

CAUCASIAN CARPET

Kuba, probably eighteenth century

SIZE	96 x 200 in.
	(244 x 508 cm.)
WARP	Wool, tan-brown interplied barber pole, Z2S, alternate warps depressed
WEFT	Wool, light red, Z, 2 shoots and singles
PILE	Wool, Z, Turkish knot (h. 8½, v. 8–8½), 64 to 72 knots per square inch
SELVEDGES	2 bundles of 2 ends wrapped
ENDS	Repaired, mixed-fiber fringe added
CONDITION	Good, firm weave, top portion rewoven

This field design, employing elements from Persian prototypes arranged in offset and vertical alternation, was familiar from India to the Caucasus in the eighteenth and early nineteenth centuries. Leaf and lotus palmettes and large floral roundels alternate with forked arabesque or lily forms on angular stems. The quite unusual light ground border shows hyacinth motifs repeated right to left and reversed alternately. The guards carry a reciprocal pattern of trefoils.

   This example well illustrates the difficulties facing students of carpets. In two recent publications, one author calls a carpet of this pattern eighteenth century,[1] while the other dates the same carpet to about 1600.[2]

PROVENANCE   Beshir Galleries, New York

1955-110

---

1. Erdmann (1962), pl. 6.
2. Ignace Schlosser, *The Book of Rugs, Oriental and European* (New York, 1960), p. 152, fig. 78.

45

46

CAUCASIAN CARPET

Probably early nineteenth century

SIZE	84 x 122 in.
	(213 x 310 cm.)
WARP	Wool, tan-brown interplied, Z2S, depressed
WEFT	Wool, dyed light red, Z, 2 shoots with fat singles at 3-inch to 5-inch intervals
PILE	Wool, Z, Turkish knot (h. 8, v. 8½–9), 69 to 72 knots per square inch
SELVEDGES	Overcast, not original
ENDS	Cut and repaired, mixed-fiber fringe added
CONDITION	Lower border repaired with strip of vertically woven border (center portion)

In this carpet the rather bland coloring, the discreet arrangement of the field, and the unusual border are features which refute a date earlier than the nineteenth century. Vertical rows of rectangular flame palmettes crowned by halo-like motifs alternate in the field with symmetrical palmettes linked vertically by hexagonal and quatrefoil devices. The design of feathery, reciprocating trefoils, enclosed within conventional trefoil guards, does not appear to be a characteristic Caucasian border.

PROVENANCE   Beshir Galleries, New York

1955-487

46

47

CAUCASIAN CARPET

Kuba, probably nineteenth century

SIZE	68 x 118 in.
	(173 x 274 cm.)
WARP	Wool, natural and some barber pole, Z2S, depressed
WEFT	Wool, reddish, Z, 2 shoots with Z3S fat singles at intervals
PILE	Wool and some natural cotton, Turkish knot (h. 7–8, v. 8), 56 to 64 knots per square inch
SELVEDGES	Repaired, overcast
ENDS	No fringe, no apron, overcast repairs
CONDITION	Good, firm weave, minor repairs to border

Stylized palmettes of basically the same design and scale in strong, vibrant colors cover the field. Erdmann points out that ". . . cloth patterns are carried over successfully to the carpets," and both this example and No. 46 resemble woven-pattern textiles in their offset, regular repeats.[1] Stiffly drawn angular palmettes also appear in Caucasian flat-woven (*kilim*) carpets. The border pattern of octagonal and *harshang* motifs has been identified by Beattie as similar to that in nineteenth-century dragon Soumaks in Trebizond and Westminster Abbey, all of which are perhaps based on borders like that shown in a sixteenth- or seventeenth-century Bergamo carpet in the Türk ve Islam Museum in Istanbul.[2]

PROVENANCE   Beshir Galleries, New York

1954-62

---

1. Erdmann (1962), p. 46, figs. 115 and 116.
2. This carpet, illustrated in Erdmann (1970), fig. 120, was called to my attention by Charles Ellis.

47

48

CAUCASIAN DESIGN CARPET
Possibly made in Istanbul, probably nineteenth century

SIZE	74 x 167 in.
	(234 x 424 cm.)
WARP	Wool, natural barber pole, Z2S, level
WEFT	Wool, ivory, Z, 2 and 3 shoots
PILE	Wool, Z, Turkish knot (h. 10, v. 11), 110 knots per square inch
SELVEDGES	Overcast, brown wool
ENDS	No apron, short warp fringe (natural, brown plied)
CONDITION	Good; close, even weave shows normal wear with no indication of chemical washing or artificial abrasion as in fake rugs

Arthur Upham Pope in 1925 wrote: "The obscure and difficult history of Oriental carpets will never be properly deciphered unless there is a more frank and vigorous give and take among the scholars in the field."[1] In his article Pope used an illustration of this carpet[2] which in the intervening years has received its share of the vigorous controversy he advocated. The colors are bright and exceptionally uniform and the condition good, several worn areas having been skillfully mended. Together with a questionable type and placement of design motifs, these features have induced specialists in recent years to call it a forgery, to date it as late as the 1930s, and to question its Caucasian provenance. Testimony in favor of Caucasian origin and the earlier date are that the carpet was thought to have sufficient age and merit to be included in three major Caucasian rug exhibitions[3] and that Pope included it in his article, which was a scholarly attempt to establish the provenance of the so-called dragon carpets as Caucasian rather than Armenian. Pope may have seen only a photograph, rather than the

---

1. "The Myth of the Armenian Dragon Carpets," *Jahrbuch der Asiatischen Kunst* 2 (1925): 158.

2. Ibid., pl. 94, fig. 4 (owned by Charles E. Gibson, Boston).

3. The Art Institute of Chicago, 1947; *A Loan Exhibition of Dragon Rugs* (Washington, D.C.: Textile Museum, 1948), no. 34 (lent by Karekin Beshir); Maurice S. Dimand, *Peasant and Nomad Rugs of Asia* (New York: Asia House Galleries, 1961), pp. 56, 78, fig. 15.

48

actual carpet, before writing his article in 1925; for if the carpet were modern, it would surely have seemed new when he published it as "18th Century."[4]

We are told that natural dyes fade or soften in hue, whereas chemical (aniline) colors change out of hue.[5] Owned and exhibited by Colonial Williamsburg for the last eleven years and almost fifty years after its publication by Pope, the carpet is still in pristine condition, not having faded badly or drastically changed in hue as in fake rugs (see No. 49). So, the questions remain: Is this, as seems likely, a nineteenth-century descendant of the so-called dragon carpets made in the Caucasus, as its prototypes were? Is this a reproduction of a Caucasian carpet design, made, as has been suggested, probably in European Turkey (Istanbul)?[6] Or is it a forgery made in the first quarter of this century in eastern Europe, where many forgeries are known to have been produced?

PROVENANCE   Beshir Galleries, New York

1962-314

---

4. Pope, "Dragon Carpets," pl. 94, no. 4.
5. George Hewitt Myers, *Textile Museum: Workshop Notes*, No. 5 (Washington, D.C.: the Museum, June 1952).
6. Charles Grant Ellis to the author, March 11, 1973.

49

CAUCASIAN FORGERY

Probably made in Europe (Balkans), about 1930

SIZE	81 x 161 in.
	(205 x 409 cm.)
WARP	Wool, natural, ends dipped yellow, Z2S, alternate ends depressed
WEFT	Wool, tan, 2–3 shoots after each row of knots
PILE	Wool, Turkish knot (h. 8, v. 9), 72 knots per square inch
SELVEDGES	Plain weave over four ends, original faded gray-blue
ENDS	Narrow apron and short warp fringe of faded yellow
CONDITION	Wear consistent over entire area, appears to have been manually and chemically aged

When a comparison is made with early Caucasian rugs, the colors

49

and design layout reveal discrepancies which indicate that this example is an outright forgery.[1]

Early in this century the manufacture of fake carpets obviously became a profitable business and many examples have, in recent years, been found in collections in Europe and America. Erdmann relates the "unmasking" of several such forgeries and remarks in some detail on this manufacture and the area in which it was carried on. He points out that ". . . first examples of really good fakes are nearly always accepted as genuine. Suspicion is not aroused until the third or fourth piece appears by which time sufficient material exists to prove the deception."[2]

This rug with its rather strange colors had been in the Williamsburg collection for several years before it was pronounced a fake by Charles Ellis. He had seen a number of similar carpets with designs that appeared to have been based on quarter-plate photographs or fragments of seventeenth-century Caucasian carpets. The colors, which in the beginning had been as carefully matched to the original as possible, have now changed completely out of hue; they bear no resemblance to the seventeenth- and eighteenth-century Caucasian palette. The design has been incorrectly drafted to repeat mirror fashion, while in the ancient rugs[3] the motifs repeat in "a progressive arrangement: that is, they were intended to be seen from one direction only."[4]

The fact that this carpet was purchased in 1957 from a reputable dealer, on the recommendation of a specialist, indicates that carpet forgeries are apt to continue on the market and to deceive the unsuspecting unless they are more generally publicized than they have been heretofore.

Erdmann says that "Half the fun would go out of carpet collecting if there were no fakes or forgeries or at least no wrongly attributed pieces."[5] However, many black sheep might be unearthed, the distinctions between the genuine and the fake, the original and the copy, would be better understood, and questions of date and provenance could be more accurately resolved if the many carpets now reposing in museum storerooms were published.

1957-35

1. A distinction should be made between antique rugs which have considerable repairs and reknotting (see No. 34), late copies or adaptations of early rug patterns where there has been no apparent intention to deceive (see No. 48), and the outright fake in which the workmanship and technique are skillful, and the ageing methods employed are expert enough to give convincing results.

2. Erdmann (1970), p. 81.

3. Bode-Kühnel, p. 62, fig. 38, illustrates the type of so-called dragon carpet which could have been the design source for this fake.

4. Ibid., p. 71.

5. Erdmann (1970), p. 85.

Bibliography

BEATTIE, MAY H. "The Burrell Collection of Oriental Rugs." *Oriental Art* 7 (1961), No. 4, p. 3.

————. *The Rug in Islamic Art*. Leeds: Leeds City Art Gallery and Temple Newsam House, 1964.

————. *The Thyssen-Bornemisza Collection of Oriental Rugs*. Switzerland, 1972. Castagnola, Switz.: the Collection, 1972.

BELLINGER, LOUISA. "Textile Analysis: Pile Techniques in Egypt and the Near East." Part 4, *Textile Museum: Workshop Notes*. Paper No. 12. Washington, D.C.: the Museum, December 1955.

BODE, WILHELM VON, and ERNST KÜHNEL. *Antique Rugs from the Near East*. Translated by Charles Grant Ellis, 4th rev. edn. Berlin and Braunschweig: Klinkhardt & Biermann, 1958.

CHICAGO ART INSTITUTE. *An Exhibition of Antique Oriental Rugs*. Chicago: the Institute, 1947.

DILLEY, ARTHUR URBANE. *Oriental Rugs and Carpets*. Revised by Maurice S. Dimand. Philadelphia: Lippincott, 1959.

DIMAND, MAURICE S. *The Ballard Collection of Oriental Rugs in the City Art Museum of St. Louis*. St. Louis: New Haven, Yale University Press, 1935.

————. *Peasant and Nomad Rugs of Asia*. New York: Asia House Gallery, 1961.

———— and JEAN MAILEY. *Oriental Rugs in the Metropolitan Museum of Art*. New York: the Museum, 1973.

ERDMANN, KURT. *Oriental Carpets: An Essay on Their History*. Translated by Charles Grant Ellis. New York: Universe Books, 1962.

————. *Seven Hundred Years of Oriental Carpets*. Translated by May H. Beattie and Hildegard Herzog; edited by Hanna Erdmann. London: Faber & Faber, 1970.

ELLIS, CHARLES GRANT. "Kirman's Heritage in Washington: Vase Rugs in the Textile Museum," *Textile Museum Journal* 2, No. 3, (December 1968), pp. 17–34.

————. "Mixed Thoughts on Oriental Carpets." *Catalogue of The Delaware Antiques Show*. Wilmington, 1969.

————. "Some Compartment Designs for Carpets, and Herat," *Textile Museum Journal* 1, No. 4 (December, 1965), pp. 42–56.

EMERY, IRENE. *The Primary Structures of Fabrics*. Washington, D.C.: Textile Museum, 1966.

ETTINGHAUSEN, RICHARD. *From Persia's Ancient Looms*. Washington: Textile Museum, 1972.

"The European Carpet," *CIBA Review*. No. 23, 1959.

FORMENTON, FABIO. *Oriental Rugs and Carpets*. Translated by Pauline L. Phillips. London and New York: Hamlyn, 1972.

GOODWIN, MARY R. M. "Carpets, Carpeting, Floor Cloths, Rugs." MS report, Colonial Williamsburg Research Department, 1960, rev. 1966.

HACKENBROCH, YVONNE. *English and Other Needlework, Tapestries, and Textiles in the Irwin Untermyer Collection*. Cambridge: Harvard University Press, 1960.

HAWLEY, WALTER A. *Oriental Rugs*. London: John Lane, 1913.

HUGHES, THERLE. *English Domestic Needlework 1660–1860*. New York: Macmillan, 1961.

JACOBS, BERTRAM. *Axminster Carpets (Hand-Made) 1755–1957*. Leigh-on-Sea, England: F. Lewis, 1970.

JACOBY, HEINRICH. *How to Know Oriental Carpets and Rugs*. London: Allen & Unwin, 1962.

———. "Materials Used in the Making of Carpets." in *A Survey of Persian Art*, vol. 3, edited by Arthur U. Pope. New York: Oxford University Press, 1938.

KENDRICK, A. F. *English Decorative Fabrics of the 16th to 18th Centuries*. Benfleet, Essex, England: F. Lewis, 1934.

——— and C. E. C. TATTERSALL. *Hand-Woven Carpets, Oriental and European*, 2 vols. New York: Benn Brothers, 1922.

LANDREAU, ANTHONY H., and W. R. PICKERING. *From the Bosporus to Samarkand, Flat-Woven Rugs*. Washington: Textile Museum, 1969.

MARTIN, FREDRIK R. *A History of Oriental Carpets before 1800*. Vienna: F. R. Martin, 1908.

MASON, FRANCES NORTON, ed. *John Norton & Sons, Merchants of London and Virginia*. Richmond: Dietz Press, 1937.

MAYORCAS, M. J. *English Needlework Carpets, Sixteenth to Nineteenth Centuries*. Leigh-on-Sea, England: F. Lewis, 1963.

McMULLAN, JOSEPH V. *Islamic Carpets*. New York: Near Eastern Art Research Center, 1965.

———. "The Turkey Carpet in Early America," *Antiques* 65 (March 1954), pp. 220–23.

MUMFORD, JOHN KIMBERLY. *Oriental Rugs*. New York: Scribner's, 1900.

MYERS, GEORGE HEWITT. *Textile Museum: Workshop Notes*. Paper No. 5. Washington, D.C.: the Museum, June 1952.

PAGE, RUTH COX. "English Carpets and Their Use in America," *Connecticut Antiquarian* 19 (June 1967), pp. 16–25.

PEREZ, ELIA. *Oriental Rugs and Textiles: The Perez Collection*. Leigh-on-Sea, England: F. Lewis, 1953.

"Pile Carpets of the Ancient Orient," *CIBA Review*. No. 15, 1938.

POPE, ARTHUR UPHAM, "Oriental Rugs as Fine Art, 1. The Aesthetic Value of the Best Types," *International Studio* 76 (November 1922), pp. 164–76.

———, ed., and PHYLLIS ACKERMAN, asst. ed. *A Survey of Persian Art from Prehistoric Times to the Present*. 6 vols. London and New York: Oxford University Press, 1938–39.

ROTH, RODRIS. *Floor Coverings in 18th-Century America*. Washington: Smithsonian Institution, 1967.

SARRE, FRIEDRICH, and HERMANN TRENKWALD. *Old Oriental Carpets*. Translated by A. F. Kendrick, 2 vols. Vienna and Leipzig: Anton Schroll, 1926–29.

SCHLOSSER, IGNACE. *The Book of Rugs, Oriental and European*. Translated from the German. New York: Crown, 1963.

SCHURMANN, ULRICH. *Caucasian Rugs*. Munich: Klinkardt & Biermann, n.d.

SYLVESTER, DAVID, and MAY H. BEATTIE. *Islamic Carpets from the Collection of Joseph V. McMullan*. London: The Arts Council of Great Britain, Hayward Gallery, 1972.

TATTERSALL, C. E. C. *Notes on Carpet Knotting and Weaving*. London: H. M. Stationery Office, 1955.

———. *A History of British Carpets*. Benfleet, Essex, England: F. Lewis, 1934.

———. *A History of British Carpets*. Revised by Stanley Reed. Leigh-on-Sea: F. Lewis, 1966.

TOMLINSON, CHARLES. *The Useful Arts and Manufactures of Great Britain*, First Series. London: Society for Promoting Christian Knowledge, n.d.

Index

ENGLISH AND ORIENTAL CARPETS AT WILLIAMSBURG
was composed in Monotype Bembo by Heritage Printers, Inc., Charlotte, North Carolina,
and printed by Lebanon Valley Offset Company Inc., Annville, Pennsylvania on Oxford's
Starflex paper. The binding was by Haddon Craftsmen, Scranton, Pennsylvania.
The designer was Richard Stinely.